In Every Tongue

··

The Racial & Ethnic Diversity
of the Jewish People

In Every Tongue

The Racial & Ethnic Diversity of the Jewish People

Diane Kaufmann Tobin
Gary A. Tobin, Ph.D.
& Scott Rubin

Foreword by Lewis Gordon, Ph.D.

Institute for Jewish &
Community Research

San Francisco, 2005

Substantial discounts on bulk quantities are available to corporations, professional associations, and other organizations.

Contact information for the Institute for Jewish & Community Research —
Phone — (415) 386-2604
Fax — (415) 386-2060
Email — info@JewishResearch.org
Web — www.JewishResearch.org

Design & Production — Scott Hummel
Photography — Stuart Brinin
Printing — Master Color Printing, Roseville, CA

Library of Congress Catalog Card Number: 2005920903
ISBN: 1-893671-01-1

This book is printed on 80# chlorine-free, archival paper using all vegetable-based inks. The paper was manufactured using sustainably harvested eucalyptus pulp.

PRINTED IN THE UNITED STATES OF AMERICA
09 08 07 06 05   5 4 3 2 1

Contents

Tables and Figures

Dedication

In Every Tongue is dedicated to our past and our ancestors. We celebrate the life of Patricia Solomon, born in Jamaica, who was deeply committed to the Jewish people. She passed away in January 2004. She was the loving mother of Lewis Gordon, a woman of strength, compassion, and generosity. She engaged in daily *mitzvot*, taking care of those in need around her.

In Every Tongue is also dedicated to new life and the future, to Jonah Kaufmann Tobin and Zeke Rubin-Moore, full of energy, optimism, and imagination. They are the inspiration for our research about diverse Jews and our community-building efforts. They, and others, are the hope of the Jewish people.

Patricia Solomon

*Zeke Rubin-Moore (left) &
Jonah Kaufmann Tobin*

Acknowledgements

We would like to thank all the participants of the national study of ethnic and racial diversity of the Jewish population for their courage and trust in sharing their life stories.

We would also like to thank all the participants of the Bay Area Be'chol Lashon community-building and evaluation efforts, especially Denise Davis, M.D., Booker Holton, Ph.D., and the entire Advisory Committee.

This work would not be possible without the community leaders from around the world who attend the annual Be'chol Lashon International Think Tank. Their life experiences and insights enrich our analysis and inform policy implications.

The success of Be'chol Lashon is the result of the collective efforts of the adjunct faculty, research associates, and dedicated staff of the Institute for Jewish & Community Research. In particular, Danielle Meshorer tirelessly navigates the myriad details necessary for the research and community-building efforts. Staff members Alexander Karp, Ph.D., Kathy Candito, Jenna Ferer, Alexis Kushner, Kathleen Rose, and Dennis Ybarra provided continuous support, good humor, and plain hard work, without which this book would not be possible. Over the past five years, others, including Meryle Weinstein, Ph.D., Patricia Lin, Ph.D., Margot Meitner, and Hilary Kaplan, have made significant contributions for which we are grateful.

We also deeply appreciate Sarah, Aryeh, and Mia Weinberg and Amy and Adam Tobin, who can always be counted on to lend their time, helping hands, and emotional encouragement to this work.

We gratefully acknowledge the vision and confidence of our financial supporters. In particular, the Righteous Persons Foundation, Steve and Maribelle Leavitt, and Al and Gail Engleberg were instrumental in the support of our research and this publication.

Your descendants shall be the dust of the earth; you shall spread out to the west and to the east, to the north and to the south.

Genesis 28:14

Foreword by *Lewis Gordon*

"Is she a Jewess?"

So asked my Uncle Puppa, my maternal grandmother's brother (Lionel, but nearly no one lives by his or her given name in the Caribbean), upon meeting my wife Jane during a visit to Ocho Rios, Jamaica.

My mother nodded, "Yes."

Jane was charmed by the irony of the meeting. A daughter of white Jewish South Africans, she grew up in a normative world of Eastern European Jews that was transformed into a multiracial Jewish world upon our meeting and subsequent marriage. She found herself in two worlds—a world of her own community's views of Jews as white and the almost invisible world of Jews of color, a world that she has come to see as not only larger than she had imagined but also more diverse. It is not, after all, as though the ancient brown and black peoples of the kingdoms of Judea simply disappeared and one day, nearly two thousand years later, woke up white. That my uncle was asking my mother if Jane was really a Jew meant that my wife's authenticity should not be presumed simply because she was also white.

My uncle explained how his maternal grandmother was a Jew from Scotland. Fleeing persecution and seeking a better life in the late nineteenth century, she and other relatives came to Jamaica to start a coconut-processing business. They found themselves on an island in which, much to the chagrin of the British Empire, race mixing was more common than acknowledged, and, in what is in fact the tradition of many (if not most) of our Jewish ancestors, they quickly began a process of miscegenation that did not privilege only the dominant group. My great-grandfather, for instance, was a tall, very dark-skinned black man with very little education. He and my maternal great-grandmother had met under the unfortunate circumstance of her having been stood up by the man with whom she was expecting to elope. My great-grandfather, nearly thirty years her senior, took her back to her parents and fell in love with her on that walk home. They were married and lived together for the next sixty years. My great-grandfather passed away after his 100th year. My great-grandmother was left with an impossible void. How does one live on after such a lifelong love? After visiting her children, grandchildren, and great-grandchildren, my great-grandmother, even if not consciously, decided to die. Six months after my great-grandfather's death, she fulfilled her wish. I was sixteen. I was fortunate to have had time with them.

Uncle Puppa explained that our family was Jewish, but some of us oscillated between Catholicism and Judaism. Although he knew he was a Jew, much of his knowledge of Judaism was limited to a few rituals in his childhood home, despite the fact that there were and continue to be several synagogues in Jamaica. (The oldest in the Anglo Caribbean, the Shaare Tzedek synagogue, built in 1654, is in Barbados.) My uncle fully embraced his Judaism after a visit to London. He stumbled on a Sephardic *shul*, where he worshiped until returning to Jamaica.

"Did you know we're Jews?"

Such a strange question. I have heard it at different times through the years of my childhood. My mother informed me and my brother Mark of our being Jews as far back as I can remember. (My brother Robert was, unfortunately, separated from the rest of the family between the ages of three and eleven, and, although Jewish by birth, knew only a Christian existence up to that point. He insists on no religious or ethnic identity beyond simply being black and Jamaican. Mark, on the other hand, lives as a Jamaican Jew, and he goes by the surname of Solomon, our mother's maiden name.) But our being Jews in the Caribbean offered the perspective of a world in which everything we held as normal everyday life was turned upside down when we immigrated to the United States. In Jamaica, my mother was a black woman descended from two lines of Jews—one from Europe, the other from the geographical heart of Jewish identity, Jerusalem. My mother's patrilineal line was the Solomons, who migrated to Jamaica in the late nineteenth century, before the dream of a Jewish homeland had been fulfilled. I met some of those relatives over the years. I remember thinking that they simply looked like light- and brown-skinned Jamaicans, which made sense since the Caribbean is full of people who are mixtures that, in many ways, match those we find today in North Africa and the Middle East. My favorite memory, however, is of an old painting of my mother's paternal grandfather: There he was with the most wonderful smile, a celebration of life, an embodiment both worldly and loving. I also saw something in that portrait that echoed the spiritual sentiments of my family. None of us saw being Jewish as a sign of sorrow or shame or anxiety but, as I once heard Rabbi Capers Funnye of Beth Shalom B'nai Zaken Ethiopian Hebrew Congregation in Chicago declare, as a blessing.

To understand Jamaican Jews, one needs to understand how religious identity is manifested in the Caribbean. Take, for example, Jamaican Christians. They are in many ways different from those in North America. Many live a dual reality as they practice forms of traditional African religions, especially Obeah, at home, in secret retreats, or, in some cases, in public in a mixture with European Christianity, as with Voodoo in Haiti. They are, in short, used to people living dual religious identities.

Many Jamaican Jews are similar. A creolization of our identity as Jamaicans enabled us to move through communities without the violence of religious bigotry. This was so, I suspect, because, in spite of all the efforts of the British—and before them the Spanish—to make the island a white world, the resisting black masses created a creolized world that pointed to an ever-present possibility of black normativity. Black family gatherings, for instance, nearly always revealed a profound level of racial and social mixture. In the Caribbean, this meant that one's immediate and extended family consisted of nearly every group—those of more immediate African descent (from all regions) to those of Asian (Eastern, Southern, and Western), European (Northern and Mediterranean), indigenous South American ancestry, as well as varieties of people from North America who settled in. With such mixtures, one's family identity has much room for different religious affiliations. This attitude is the way of life on most of the islands with a strong black identity.

In places where the national identity encourages a great distance from being black, stories of intolerance abound. I recall a conversation with a good friend from Cuba who became an Orthodox rabbi. Although we both have stories of at-home Jewish identities versus public ones, his experience was of a family who *had to* remain hidden for generations because of the dangers of being publicly Jewish in a Spanish Catholic-centered Cuba. (He did not grow up in Castro's Cuba.) Ironically, my family neither asserted nor hid our Jewish identity, because we didn't live as though being Jewish made any difference.

Being a Jew changed for me, however, through encounters that occasioned much reflection. The first was migrating to the United States at the age of nine. We lived in the South Bronx, in New York City. The populations were mostly Italian Catholics, Puerto Rican Catholics, and black Catholics and Protestants. Although there are white people in Jamaica, they are not like whites in the United States. American whites (and sometimes blacks) seem to have an obsession with asserting how *white* they are. For me, then, in 1971, at the age of nine, processes of Americanization began. In elementary school, I learned both what a "nigger" was and how it felt to be called such. I discovered the limits on mobility, that there were places one could not walk, that there were public facilities that one could not use, simply because one was black. In most of these cases, it was not because of some law that was still active on the books. There were simply communities of white people who saw my presence in "their" schools, parks, and streets as an act of pollution. My first encounter with anti-Semitism also occurred during that period. White Christian children would throw pennies on the ground. "For the Jews," they would say. I asked them why they did that. "Jews are cheap and greedy," they would say. When I told them I was a Jew, they either didn't believe me or simply retorted, "Then pick up the penny." I got in many fights during that period. As I later chronicled in my book, *Her Majesty's Other Children*, I nearly always fought against racist attacks, either because I was black or because my opponents mistook me for a member of a different ethnic group, like Puerto Rican.

I lived during those years in a world that was best exemplified by the three gangs who controlled their territories in the Bronx: the Black Spades, the White Spears, and the Chingalings. The racial identities of the first two are obvious. The Chingalings were a Puerto Rican biker gang with extraordinary business acumen, having purchased several buildings. In the midst of all this, I occasionally met *white* Jewish children. Most of the children were a variety of Catholics. Such was the South Bronx.

Eventually, fire from a neighbor's apartment forced us to move to the eastern areas of the Bronx, near Laconia and Pelham Parkway. Although a mostly Italian Catholic area, there were many synagogues, and I began to meet more white Jewish children with whom I played. What I never mentioned to those friends, and I suspect what most Jews of color who find themselves in similar situations keep silent, is that *I* was going through a shift in perspective from meeting *them*. How could these people be Jews when every *actual* Jew I had known up to that point was a person of color? Sure, I had seen the European portraits of figures in the Hebrew Bible, but even as a child I knew that these were simply portraits and interpretations of *Europeans*, not ancient Hebrews. Why were most of the Jewish children I was meeting no different in appearance from New York Italians and Germans? My mother's brothers would bring books home that explained about Judaism and Islam in Africa, a history, unfortunately, of which most white American Jews seem to have been unaware. Much became clear through my friendship with my childhood best friend, Michael.

Mike was a child of an Ashkenazi Jewish mother and a Catholic Italian father. When asked about his background, he often simply said, "Italian." I met him one day when, walking home in the sixth grade, I heard a squeaky voice call out to me from a white convertible Cadillac: "Hey, you're in my class! Would you like a ride home?" He explained that his mother was in the grocery store purchasing a snack. She soon came out, a classic example of life in the early 1970s: Her hair was dyed blond and left flowing, she wore a white tube top and the tightest pair of black pants I had ever seen; and in her hand was a bag of pork rinds.

"This is my friend Lewis," said Mike.

"Hello," said his mom with a bright smile while munching her snack. "Would you like some pork rinds? They're *really good!*" Through Mike I learned of a world of white American Jewish youth that was radically different from my Caribbean understanding of Judaism. White American Jews struck me as people who, by virtue of being white, could be whatever they wanted to be. My friend Mike had both a bar mitzvah *and* a confirmation ceremony as a Catholic! I recall, many years later, visiting his Jewish maternal grandmother, who insisted that he try her latest batch of homemade kosher pickles, and then visiting his paternal grandmother that evening, who, while serving an enormous Italian meal replete with pork and mozzarella cheese, gasped with wonder as she noticed that Mike, standing next to her portrait of a very Italian Jesus, looked "like the Father!"

I lived for many years as a secular Jew, pretty much the way many white Jews in New York City did, but I always had a relationship of curiosity to religious questions.[1] Why, for instance, did having a religious identity make so many people so zealous? This puzzled me, I have come to realize, because I didn't see Judaism as a religion. The world I am from was one in which one was simply born a Jew—end of story. Such a view enabled me to live as a Jew while knowing very little about Judaism beyond how it presents itself in the *Tanakh* and what my mother and grandmother and uncles told me. I knew nothing of Talmudic writings nor Hasidic tales.

All my girlfriends in my adolescent years were African American and Afro-Caribbean Christians or Dominican and Puerto Rican Catholics. It wasn't until my early twenties that I had a girlfriend, Ruth, who was descended from Russian Jews. She, in many ways, exemplified something that is not often written about in studies of white Jews in New York City: she was lower working class. She lived on the Grand Concourse, an area that for a long time was full of such Jews. (A decade later, when I visited Prague,

I saw that much of what I thought was Eastern European Jewish culture was, in fact, a blend of Jewish and Eastern European culture. Walking down the streets of Prague, one could almost forget that one was not walking on the Grand Concourse in the Bronx.) Ruth did not grow up going to synagogue, and she did not have a bat mitzvah. At no moment, however, did she doubt that she was a Jew. In short, although she was white, she and I were a lot alike.

My first wife, Lisa, was an Afro-Native American Christian. (We later divorced.) Our children, Mathieu and Jenny, were informed about being of Jewish descent through me, and while I was married to her, I continued the practice of indifference to religion ... until she began to stress a more Christian identity in the children. I began to realize that I was, in many ways, like many other secular Jews worldwide: we claim not to be interested in religion, but in truth, whereas we may not actively pursue our Jewish religious identity, we *strongly object* to our children having a Christian one. I began to realize that Judaism was calling to me in ways that I was failing to admit.

The story was different with my current wife Jane, but it was no doubt affected by my also having come to realize certain things about who I was and continue to be. When I met Jane, we talked much about how we felt about Judaism, about being Jews who were at that time not as active about what it meant to be who we were. Jane had, however, grown up taking very seriously what it meant to be a *religious* Jew and a *political* Jew. She grew up going to shul and Jewish socialist camp. She took seriously her teachings from a charismatic rabbi committed to social justice, and she reflected much on the teachings involved in her bat mitzvah and had even sought confirmation as a Jew and considered eventually becoming a rabbi. The crisis for her in Judaism was more connected to the contradictions she saw in American Jewish life: the naked pursuit of assimilation with American whiteness while asserting a cultural difference.

We opted for a Jewish wedding or *kiddushin*, which brought relatives together on a beautiful spring day in a celebration of what, according to Judaism, is an affirmation of what already existed. Some years later, I found myself in a political debate with a white secular Jew. The debate, ironically, emerged from my intervening to challenge the presumption, in an online debate on Israeli and Palestinian politics, that Israelis were an exclusively white Jewish population versus populations of color (the Palestinians). I argued that most Jews living in Israel could be characterized as people of color and that there are Jews worldwide who both do not and *cannot* be identified as white. After all, most Israelis have Sephardic and Middle Eastern heritage. Why, the challenger posed, would Jews of color want to acknowledge their Jewish background? I was confronted here with a new kind of question, one which I had not seen broached to white Jews, but which I'm sure some might have faced: *Why do you choose to continue being a Jew?*

An odd feature of the question is the presumption that choice is somehow more a question for a black Jew than it is for a white one. Something insidious lay beneath it, for I suspected that the challenger did not treat his Jewish identity as something over which he had a choice.

In my reply, I pointed out that I had spent most of my life as a secular Jew, as someone who adamantly did not want to be involved in Jewish *religious* life, because I saw a double standard imposed upon African and African Diasporic Jews that was not faced by white Jews. Black Jews had to be religious and meet all kinds of criteria that white Jews, in fact, did not have to meet. White Jews, in other words, could be secular. The underlying theme was that white Jews are *really Jews no matter what*. So, I had consciously focused on being a born Jew as a fight against that prejudice.

But then I had children. It became clear to me that there was something shallow about simply saying that one is a Jew by birth.

What should, in other words, being a Jew *mean* to my children? It struck me that when I think about what being of African descent means to me, it involves teaching my children about Africa and about the many aspects of being African as it has manifested itself in the New World. It involves understanding how to value being black, how to value being respected as a human being and the many things offered culturally, for instance, about being born in Jamaica. Yes, there were aspects of Jamaican Jewish rituals, unique mixtures, that survived, but my children are not only of Jamaican Jewish descent. They are also of South African Jewish descent, and in turn they are of Russian and German Jewish descent. Jane and I had begun to observe some Jewish rituals, including attending shul during Jewish holidays and, although not all the time, celebrating Shabbat in order to present an enriched understanding of the many rivers, as Langston Hughes put it, flowing through their veins and into our family's collective memory.[2] I pointed out that an unexpected feature of being involved in such activities with our children afforded important reflection and understanding of the beauty of Jewish life—not a misguided notion of its "perfection." The beauty consists of the complex, often contradictory messages that present a worldview on problems of life and death, on proper humility toward things genuinely great, and an outrage against things profoundly unjust. I wrote of Pesach and of how profoundly powerful it is to reflect on slavery as a New World black Jew, that it is much like an Eastern European Jew reflecting on the Shoah in relation to the various Inquisitions—the realization of *the recent* is almost overwhelming.

Children. Family. In many ways, that brings us to the heart of the matter. Jane and I often reflected on who we were, because we were aware of what we hoped to become. For us, much of that is connected to the possibilities we saw in each other's unyielding sense of the love that binds us. There is more that brings us together. The reader may notice that throughout this autobiography of my Jewish family's life, I have constantly presented the question of birthright. That is not, however, as many of us know, the fundamental problem of Judaism, a problem that offers a paradox: even born Jews *must become Jews.*

Judaism is hard work. It is no wonder that the great Christian thinker Søren Kierkegaard often turned to the Hebrew Bible when he complained about complacency and a lack of passion in modern life. Judaism demands much from those who uphold its laws, and it does so without the promise of an afterlife. Judaism demands good deeds, but it demands that the good-doer expect no recognition for his or her actions. And it goes on and on.

A terrible feature of contemporary life is the need for a neat, saccharine past. We live, in many ways, in a world of escapism where many of us would like, simply by an act of choice, to achieve a radical conversion of *everything.* I have always found such a mentality evasive of reality. Who we are is also a function of things that we cannot change but that we should try to understand. It is the ambiguity of adult existence, what it is to be placed between having life given to us without our having played a role in the matter and awaiting our death in a way that challenges us to live a meaningful life.

"We're Jews, you know?" Those words came from my mother during my childhood.

In 2004, I sat at a table of food and wine for Pesach without my mother any longer walking the earth. The love of friends, many of whom knew her and loved her dearly, offered sustenance during such difficult times.

In a plot in Hastings on the Hudson, in Westchester, New York, there is a tombstone with my mother's name with the Star of David to the left. My mother died in an automobile accident in early January of that year. Although burning *yahrzeit* candles at the loss of a loved one is traditionally only for a week, my wife and I continue to burn candles in her memory. We cannot let her go. We read the mourner's Kaddish regularly, which reminds us that life does not belong to us and that death is a reminder of that, or we simply reflect on how valuable my mother was to us and our children and the more than 1,800 people who showed up to bid her goodbye at her funeral. In those moments of reflection, I see the unfolding of so much we shared. My mother was a woman of enormous courage. One of my memories is of her and me leaning on each other's forehead for twenty-four hours as we waited on the concrete pavement in front of the Immigration and Naturalization Service in New York City in the early winter's cold for amnesty as immigrants in 1981. In many ways, that experience was a metaphor for our relationship: we loved and depended on each other.

My mother was a feisty woman. She spoke the truth lovingly, and the love she had was for people in terms of who they were. She fought against many things evil and for everything from national politics to workers' rights at her job. She helped so many people that it was difficult for me to see how she was able to devote so much time to her children and grandchildren. Yet she did.

I have often wondered how my mother would have lived her life had she known what I have learned over the past several years about Jewish communities worldwide. Many ironic things came out at my mother's death. My stepfather, for instance, with whom I never discussed religion until we sat lamenting our loss, revealed to me that he was a born Jew, and although his father had practiced Judaism, most of his family were Catholics. An even more complicated moment was hearing from Auntie Plumber, one of my maternal grandmother's sisters. Although her children and my mother were of the same generation, none of them knew of their Jewish ancestry. When I brought it up, my aunt simply assented to its truth, telling her children, most of whom were in their mid- to late-50s, the story that her brother, Uncle Puppa, related to Jane and me just several months earlier. In many ways, my aunt, my mother, and the many members of our community I have met face the question of why should they bother to assert their Jewish identity.

I have been fortunate enough to meet communities of Jews in a variety of settings because of my work as an intellectual. When I taught at Brown University, most of my classes had one or sometimes several Jews of color. In one small seminar, eight of ten students were Jewish, although only two of the students were white. I have received letters from many Jewish communities, but none has had an effect on me as much as the community of Be'chol Lashon (In Every Tongue), a program organized by Diane and Gary Tobin of the Institute for Jewish & Community Research in San Francisco. Knowing much about the diversity of Jewish communities worldwide is one thing. Sitting in a room with nearly a hundred representatives of such communities is another matter. I participated in the 2002 Be'chol Lashon International Think Tank, where I was able to see the beautiful tapestry of Lemba Jews from South Africa, Ethiopian Jews, the Abayudaya of Uganda, Ibo (also known as Igbo, derivation of Hebrew) Jews of Nigeria, Egyptian Jews, Cuban Jews, Spanish and Portuguese Conversos who have returned to Judaism, Ashkenazi Jews, Sephardic Jews, and Israelites. Some of the participants were also Jews from mixed marriages involving Jewish mothers; others were children of Jewish men who sought connection with their Jewish family; many were "converts." I place conversion in quotation marks because many were also born Jews who felt the need to affirm their identity through practices of converting to a particular movement. Some were Asian, and others were Native American. Some were lesbians, and some were gay men. All were in active struggle *with* and *for* this way of living that we call Judaism. It became clear to me, as I participated in four days of talks and the ongoing discussions that followed over the next three years, that something *special* was being realized by this wonderful community of hope—namely, a new stage in the history of Jewish people. It is post-denominational and pan-denominational, post-racial and pan-racial. It is what Judaism has always been—we are a people.

Peoplehood involves taking seriously the diversity of Jews and the complexity of our history. It involves taking on the fallacies that have been imposed on our past in the service of a false, homogeneous identity that has encouraged bigotry. Take, for instance, the presumption of linear migration and the maintenance of racial and ethnic "purity." Standard narratives on the history of Jews would make us think that fewer than 100 people could be enslaved in Egypt for more than 500 years and that nearly 600,000 people could leave, completely intact and exactly like the original 100. Afterward, these people go through a series of colonizing intruders and eventually move, in linear fashion, into Greece and then Rome and then into Europe and then spread throughout the world looking today as they supposedly looked over the past three thousand years. By contrast, Africans went through 300 years of slavery in North America, and today are a mixed people who speak a European language and mostly follow the religions of Europe and the Middle East. In truth, people do not migrate (whether voluntarily or forced) without their descendants mixing in with the local populations over time. Whatever the people were like who went into Egypt, many of them were mixed with the other slaves in Egypt, and the community that came out of Egypt into Canaan was a creolized Egyptian/African one. When subsequent migrations were forced, it is prejudice that makes us assume that people only fled or were enslaved northward. Others went east and west and south. Other considerations, such as trade and politics, drove still others across Africa and then others across the Atlantic and Indian Oceans. In each of these instances, they developed their own ways of practicing what is the common thread that binds us. I recall asking an Iraqi student's father what kind of Jew he was. He was rightfully insulted. "I reject that nonsense," he said. "My ancestors wrote the Talmudic writings that those Ashkenazi and Sephardic Jews rest their teachings on, and they're always asking how I relate to *them!*"

Many Jews simply do not fit into single categories. And this isn't new. Many of us never have. I thank the Tobins for beginning this first step of bringing to print some of the testimonies and demographic work on who and, in a word, *what* we really are. The world of physics claims these days that the visible universe is, as it turns out, the smallest portion of the universe. The rest, the majority, is that vast, mysterious reality of invisible or dark matter. Still, knowing that it is out there humbles us at how vast reality is. In many ways, a similar message is offered by the work of the Tobins in organizing Be'chol Lashon. Their work, of which this book is a small testament, is a reminder that much about Judaism involves the question of *becoming a Jew*, which calls us to think through what this entails, what it means to raise the question of our possibility beyond simply our survival but rather to the challenge of our growth.

I close with a reflection, "Renewal of the Moon," in the presence of the moon, *Birkat Hal'vanah*, especially given the archaeological evidence of the roots of Judaism in the moon cults of the slaves of ancient Egypt, whose God, Jah or Yahweh, serves as the foundation of what was eventually born in the land of Canaan.[3]

I lift my eyes to the hills:
heaven and earth are my comforts.
By day the sun does not harm me,
by night the moon is my guide.

It renews its light
for those just beginning,
who will one day find
their own renewal.

May the moon
be as praised as the sun
and all be equal
as when we began.[4]

A Synonym for Jewish

When she was in college, Sasha[1] searched for a place to settle her identity. Like many college students, she dipped in and out of student organizations, campus affiliations, and friendships. Unlike many of her peers, though, Sasha had a myriad of choices.

Freshman year she found most of her friends among the other students on her floor in the dorm. There were, she said, "a couple of mixed people and a couple of Asian people, but mostly everyone was white." She fit in, sort of: her mother was white and Jewish, a second-generation American of Ashkenazi descent; her Catholic father was African American, Puerto Rican, and Native American. Then sophomore year she joined a black women's support group, and suddenly she found herself having to choose an identity.

The members of the group, part of the African American Student Union, told her, "If you're mixed, that's fine. We don't have any issues with that, but when you're here, you're here because you're black." At the end of the year, Sasha decided "not to continue [her affiliation with the African American Student Union] anymore because I didn't know what it was like just to choose one thing." She had never been forced to define herself into a single category.

Until that point, her identity had been comfortably fluid. Her father used to pull her out of primary school to go to pow-wows and other Indian gatherings. She attended Catholic Mass in Spanish with her babysitter and grew up speaking both Spanish and English. And, while she never became a bat mitzvah, she taught Sunday school at the Reform synagogue near her house.

The push to affiliate, to declare her allegiance to one ethnic or religious community encumbered Sasha. She tried joining the Latino group on campus, but they were interested in "what you look like, how you sound when you speak Spanish," so she moved on. She attended a few events at Hillel and occasionally held Seders and Chanukah celebrations herself, but she found that the Jewish organization "wasn't really fun." In the end, she joined the Intertribal Student Union, because, she said, "a lot of people were mixed and talked about being mixed." She had finally found her home—among those who had no specific home.

> *To be Jewish and not white is to fall outside the notion of who is a Jew held by most Americans, Jewish or not.*

Sasha's struggle to find a group with which to affiliate, while perhaps exaggerated by the complexity of her heritage, is emblematic of the way many diverse Jews seek to reconcile their multiple identities, either to themselves or to the various communities that would claim them. To be Jewish and not white is to fall outside the notion of who is a Jew held by most Americans, Jewish or not. Sasha described her own concept of the relationship between being white and being Jewish: "If people asked me what I was, I would run down my mix. I wouldn't normally say white. I would usually say Jewish, but to me that was synonymous."

Sasha is not alone. Most American Jews hardly find it necessary to think about their race or ethnicity in relationship to their identity as Jews. Like Sasha, the majority of Jews in the United

States are likely to believe that Jewish = white. Experience supports that idea: look around most synagogues in America, and you will see almost exclusively people who blend into the racial majority. And yet, some may be surprised to find that diverse Jews comprise 20% of the Jewish population in the United States.

The Demographic Study of Jews Is Difficult

Scholars, community leaders, and the public at large often inquire about the size, make-up, and location of the diverse Jewish population. The demographic study of Jews is difficult for a variety of reasons. First, some countries, like the United States, do not ask about religion in their census counts of the population. A number of groups (including many Jewish institutions) are concerned about the separation of church and state, and do not want the government inquiring about religion. Therefore, we rely on a variety of surveys to try to estimate the Jewish population, including the number of diverse Jews.[2]

Second, Jewish communities are highly dispersed. Even in communities with significant Jewish populations, people are more likely to be scattered among the general population than in previous generations. Jews also live in the suburban fringes of many metropolitan areas, far from any Jewish population center, making them difficult to locate. Finding Jewish respondents outside major metropolitan areas is an even more challenging needle-in-a-haystack endeavor.

Third, some Jews do not want to be found. When receiving an unexpected telephone call from a stranger wanting to know if they are Jewish or not, many will simply hang up the phone or even hide their identity or background. The Institute for Jewish & Community Research conducted methodological tests for its study of the Jewish population in the United States that confirm that there are many Jews that previous studies missed. Some groups of Jews are more reluctant than others to reveal their religious identity to telephone survey researchers, such as Russian Jews and Israelis in the United States. Among those people who may not be inclined to cooperate with survey researchers are those who tend to mistrust governments; who have been victims of persecution; who reject their religious identity; and who think of themselves as ethnic Jews rather than religious Jews. Both locating Jews and inducing them to reveal their religious identity complicate and compromise our ability to estimate the number of diverse Jews.

The Number of Jews in the United States

The 2002 national telephone survey conducted by the Institute for Jewish & Community Research (IJCR) estimates there are over 6 million Jews in the United States, considerably more than the 5.2 million Jews counted by the 2000 National Jewish Population Survey (NJPS) conducted by the United Jewish Communities (UJC). Our estimate of over 6 million Jews includes the same categories included in other population estimates: those who say Judaism is their religion and those who have a Jewish background (parent or upbringing).

The Institute for Jewish & Community Research survey was able to locate more Jews due to the nature of the questions and the order in which they were asked. For example, the Institute found that it was less threatening to begin the interview with a series of personal questions that inquired about ancestry rather than religious identity.

This is especially important because many American Jews think of themselves more in ethnic or cultural terms than in religious ones, and are more comfortable talking about that aspect of their identity. Other studies conducted by IJCR have shown that many Jews say, "I am not a religious Jew or a practicing Jew, but I feel Jewish. I am a cultural Jew." The discrepancy between the IJCR count of 6 million Jews and the NJPS count of 5.2 million Jews is partially due to IJCR's success in having more ethnic and cultural Jews respond to the survey.

Diverse Jews Are a Growing Population in the United States

Diversity characterizes the American Jewish community, partially through historical antecedents and partially through contemporary social forces at work. The Jewish community is growing and changing through intermarriage, conversion, and adoption. Some of the individuals entering the community via these avenues are people of color.

We estimate at least 20% of the Jewish population is racially and ethnically diverse, including African, African American, Latino (Hispanic), Asian, Native American, Sephardic, Mizrahi and mixed-race Jews by heritage, adoption, and marriage. Calculating this number is challenging and requires examining a number of different sources.

First, according to the 2002 IJCR study and the 2000 NJPS study, a little over 7% of America's 6 million Jews say that they are African American, Asian, Latino/Hispanic, or Native American or mixed-race, for a total of about 435,000 individuals. This includes 85,000 who say that they are some race other than white but do not classify themselves more specifically. Second, the NJPS 2000 found 120,000 Jewish adults living in the United States who were born in Latin America, the Middle East, Asia, and the Caribbean (not including Israel). We estimate that over half of this foreign-born population (not including children) is comprised of diverse Jews, adding another 65,000.

Third, the number of Israelis living in the United States is under great dispute, including those of diverse backgrounds. For example, the NJPS found only 70,000-93,000 Israelis living in the United States, while the most recent New York demographic study showed about 50,000 Israelis in New York alone. The U.S. Census reports almost 200,000 people who speak Hebrew at home. A 2003 study by the Israeli Foreign Ministry showed almost a half million (500,000) Israelis living in the United States.

Therefore, based on the U.S. Census, we are conservatively estimating the total number of Israelis in the United States at 200,000. Because approximately 40-50% of the population in Israel is of Mizrahi, Sephardic, and African heritage, it stands to reason that about 50% of Israelis in the United States could be Mizrahi, Sephardic, or African Jews (who are not included in the other categories listed). Therefore, we conservatively estimate that 100,000 Israelis living in the United States are of diverse backgrounds, or 1.7% of American Jews. This brings the total to 600,000 diverse Jews, or about 10% of the population.

Fourth, a question regarding Sephardic heritage was not asked in the 2000 NJPS, although the 1990 National Jewish Population Survey showed that 8% of American Jews said they were Sephardic. Is the real percentage 10%? More? We do not know, other than to surmise it is considerably higher than is reported.

The number of Jews with some Sephardic heritage is likely to be grossly underestimated in many Jewish surveys, including the NJPS. Sephardic heritage is especially apt to be lost in individuals' self-reporting. Many people do not know about their Sephardic background, especially given the propensity of different groups of Jews to intermarry over generations throughout the Diaspora. Taking into consideration all these factors, we are conservatively estimating 10% of the United States population has some Sephardic heritage, in addition to those who say their race is Latino/Hispanic. We have taken into account potential overlap in this reporting and adjusted our estimate accordingly.

Adding 600,000 Sephardic Jews or 10% of the Jewish population together with 600,000 or 10% of African American, Asian, Latino and mixed-race Jews means 1.2 million or 20% of the Jewish population in the United States is diverse. This includes individuals who have converted to Judaism, individuals who have been adopted into Jewish families and raised as Jews, the multiracial children of partnerships between Ashkenazi Jews and people of color, and those who are themselves the generational descendants of Jews of color and those of Sephardic and Mizrahi heritage. (See Table 1.)

The Potential to Grow the Jewish People

In addition to over 6 million Jews, IJCR also found some 4.2 million adults in the United States with Jewish heritage: those with a Jewish grandparent or great-grandparent, or more distant

Table 1
Population estimate of ethnically and racially diverse Jews in the United States

Population Type	Percent of U.S. Jewish Population	Individuals	Source
African American, Black, Asian, Latino or Hispanic,* Native American, mixed-race or some race other than white (non-specific)**	7.3%	435,000	National Jewish Population Survey (NJPS) 2000/ Institute for Jewish & Community Research Study (IJCR) 2002
African, South American, Middle Eastern, Asian, and Caribbean foreign-born	1.0%	65,000	NJPS 2000
Israelis with Sephardic or Mizrahi heritage	1.7%	100,000	U.S. Census 2000
Subtotal	**10.0%**	**600,000**	
Sephardic heritage***	10.0%	600,000	NJPS 1990
TOTAL (of 6 million U.S. Jews)	**20.0%**	**1,200,000**	**IJCR 2002**

* *Half of Latinos/Hispanics listed their race as white, and half did not. We accounted for overlap in our estimate.*

** *These numbers have been aggregated due to the small sample size, but the approximate breakdown is African American 1%, Asian 2%, Latino 3% and the remaining 1.3% is Native American, mixed-race and some race other than white (non-specific).*

*** *Estimate of those who are not African American, Black, Asian, Native American or mixed-race, or foreign-born and do not identify as Latino or Hispanic, adjusted from the 8% figure cited by the NJPS.*

Jewish ancestor. Of these 4.2 million, there are 700,000 people with diverse backgrounds who are not currently Jewish but are aware of a Jewish ancestor. When asked, they claim their Jewish heritage as part of their ethnic or religious identity, even if they do not answer Jewish when asked about their current primary identity. Of course, these numbers would be much larger if more people knew more about their Jewish ancestry. Many who are not currently Jewish have historical ties to Judaism but do not know about their ethnic origins. Ethnic histories over the centuries are quite complex and are lost to many. Millions of people have Jewish ancestors, especially those of Portuguese, Spanish, and African descent, but are unaware of it.

We also found a population of some 2.5 million adults who are not Jewish, but who have a connection to Judaism or the Jewish community. This includes some who are married to Jews and feel identified with the community and others who have an affinity with Judaism or Jews based on intellectual or emotional identification. They are entwined in the Jewish community but are not self-defined as Jews. This group includes some 225,000 adults—"connected non-Jews"—of diverse backgrounds who are connected to the Jewish people through marriage, friendship, extended family, community, or personal interest.

Table 2
Current Jewish and associated populations

Population Types	Total Population	Diverse Population	Percent Diverse Population
Currently Jewish	6,000,000	1,200,000	20%
Jewish Heritage	4,200,000	700,000	16%
Connected non-Jews	2,500,000	225,000	9%

Source: Surveying the Jewish Population in the United States - Part 1: Population Estimate, Part 2: Methodological Issues & Challenges, Institute for Jewish & Community Research, 2004.

Some of these individuals are on the path to conversion; they may even be living as Jews in terms of synagogue attendance or ritual observance but have not yet formally become Jews through a conversion or affirmation process. Some may practice Judaism and another religion but have not yet decided to practice only Judaism. Some are so entwined within the Jewish community that they feel Jewish, according to their own self-assessment. They participate in Jewish life and may be raising their children as Jews. (See Table 2.)

Jews of Color Are a Growing Population around the World

Finding Jews in the United States is a simple task when compared to finding individuals and groups with Jewish ancestry around the world. The sophisticated methods of survey research do not apply, and written records sometimes do not exist. Oral traditions or ritual practice are the indicators of Jewish roots and help find some people. Others do not know about their religious origins, especially those descended from ancient but now assimilated Jewish communities in Africa. Many descendants of Spanish and Portuguese Jews have no idea about their Jewish ancestry.

The potential for Jewish population growth around the world, especially in Latin America and Africa, is as significant as it is in the United States. We estimate millions of people of color who 1) have converted to Judaism; 2) have Jewish heritage; 3) who identify with Judaism; or 4) are on the path to Judaism in South Africa, Mozambique, Zimbabwe, Uganda, Nigeria, Ghana, Kenya, Burundi, and elsewhere in Africa. A community in Uganda, the Abayudaya, has been practicing Judaism for almost a hundred years. They recently went through a formal conversion with a Conservative *beit din*. Other such communities exist in India, Burma, Brazil, Peru, and around the globe.

Jewish = white, indeed.

The Jewish origins of the (growing) population of diverse Jews are complex. Like Sasha, there are many racially and ethnically diverse Jews who are born Jewish. Additionally, significant numbers of Jews marry someone who is not born Jewish. Even when the non-Jewish partner does not convert, their children may grow up with a Jewish identity, with multiple religious identities like Sasha, or with no religious identity at all.[3]

These individuals are not necessarily mixed-race. Around the world, including within the United States, there are long-established families and communities of color that have been Jewish for generations. Some people of color become Jews through formal conversion, and still others live as Jews—transforming their identity psychologically and functionally—without undertaking rites of conversion. An increasing number of people of color become Jewish when they are adopted by Jewish parents. Many, but not all, of these adopted children undergo a formal conversion while they are still minors and grow up just like other Jewish children in America.

> Numbers are important for their own sake. Despite the outcries so common in Jewish institutional circles that quality, not quantity, matters, both are important.

As with nearly every question in Jewish life, on its own each of these "paths to Judaism" has its accompanying challenges, controversies, and opportunities for change. Add to this mix the overlay of racial politics in America, and the questions become more complicated and controversial.

So why should the wider Jewish community care? First, diverse Jews already represent a substantial part of American Jewry and their numbers are increasing. The number of diverse Jews around the world is also increasing. Diverse Jews help grow the Jewish population. The potential for increasing that number—

thereby increasing our communal numbers overall—is significant and intriguing. Numbers are important for their own sake. Despite the outcries so common in Jewish institutional circles that quality, not quantity, matters, both are important. **A larger, more expansive Jewish community is healthier than a shrinking one.** Considering the number of "connected non-Jews" already in existence, as well as those Americans, including people of color, who feel free to choose or reject the religion of their birth, the Jewish community could greatly expand, perhaps by millions, if it were more open and could attract new individuals, including individuals of color. In addition to the fact that being unwelcoming violates Jewish values, Jews should cherish people in the world that they can count on for support in the face of rising anti-Semitism.

Although population growth is critical, numbers alone will not sustain the Jewish community. The depth of involvement and participation of individual Jews is also essential.

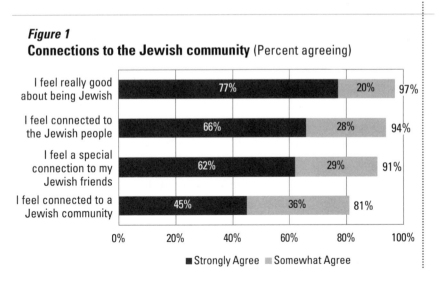

Figure 1
Connections to the Jewish community (Percent agreeing)

	Strongly Agree	Somewhat Agree	Total
I feel really good about being Jewish	77%	20%	97%
I feel connected to the Jewish people	66%	28%	94%
I feel a special connection to my Jewish friends	62%	29%	91%
I feel connected to a Jewish community	45%	36%	81%

■ Strongly Agree ■ Somewhat Agree

Source: Survey of Racially & Ethnically Diverse Jews in the United States, Institute for Jewish & Community Research, 2001.

The wider Jewish community should care about diversity because most diverse Jews are deeply identified as Jews, regardless of their path to Judaism or their degree of institutional or religious affiliation. This is a fundamental indication of a community's long-term viability. The 2001 Institute for Jewish Community Research survey of diverse Jews found that some racially and ethnically diverse Jews in the survey were ambivalent about their connection to Jewish *institutions*, but they still felt deeply connected to the Jewish *people* and the Jewish *religion*. Seventy-seven percent (77%) "strongly agreed" and 20% "somewhat agreed" (97%) with the statement, "I feel really good about being Jewish."Sixty-six percent (66%) "strongly agreed" with the statement, "I feel connected to the Jewish people," while another 28% "somewhat agreed," for a total of 94%. (See Figure 1.)

Diverse Jews tend to be more positive about being Jewish than the Jewish community as a whole and have the same or higher levels of involvement than the general Jewish population.[4] Ninety-nine percent (99%) of the respondents who volunteered to be in the study said that being Jewish was either "very important" (86%) or "somewhat important" (13%) to them. More than two-thirds of the respondents said that the following were "very important" to them: fighting anti-Semitism (76%); remembering the Holocaust (72%); and having their children be Jewish (73%). (See Figure 2.) Celebrating Jewish holidays ranks high, with 67% saying it is "very important." Like other Jews, celebrating Passover (85%) and Chanukah (83%) are most widely observed, both of which take place outside of a synagogue and usually in the company of family and friends, those who are most like oneself.

For the Jewish community to continue to thrive into coming generations, **the American Jewish community must find a way to make Judaism more meaningful to the growing numbers of disenfranchised Jews, which include younger people. Diversity is one of the keys to that future.** The American people, including

Figure 2
Attitudes about importance of Jewish practices, behaviors, and beliefs (Percent agreeing)

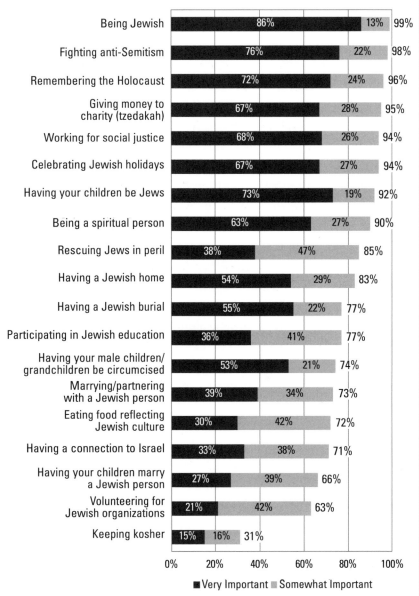

Source: *Survey of Racially & Ethnically Diverse Jews in the United States, Institute for Jewish & Community Research, 2001.*

younger Jews, are growing up in a world that believes racial or ethnic insularity to be racist and polarizing. They consider archaic a community that separates itself from other cultures. Popular music, film, and other art forms that appeal to younger people borrow freely from many cultures and no longer disguise their origins. Diversity is such an important part of American identity, that the Jewish community would be well served by acknowledging and embracing racial and ethnic diversity within its own ranks.

Diversity is also important because throughout history—and not just in Europe—Jews have struggled against persecution and discrimination. Now, sheltered within the safety of the United States, **Jews have a moral obligation to fight discrimination of all kinds, including within their own community.** This includes not only racial and ethnic discrimination (against Jews and gentiles alike), but also against unfair standards of who is a Jew. There are individuals and entire communities of color who want to be accepted and welcomed into the larger Jewish community. By their faith and by their actions, they are part of the Jewish people, and the American Jewish community has a responsibility to support and encourage their enthusiasm for Judaism. Jews have known suspicion and rejection throughout history; they should not turn those same fears against those who would be part of them.

That is not to say that anti-Semitism in the United States is non-existent. For the last several years, anti-Semitism (sometimes hidden in the form of anti-Israelism) has been rising in the United States, in Europe, and especially in the Muslim world. **Encouraging diversity within the Jewish community is one way to address the threat of anti-Semitism.** Anti-Semites portray Israel and Jews as "white colonialists," sometimes likening Israeli actions to the former South African policy of apartheid or even to Nazi practices. Those who oppose the existence of Israel often appeal to individuals of color to join together, playing a "race card" by branding Israel as a racist society. Diverse Jews, by their very existence, explode the myth of Jews as the "white race." This misrepresentation of Israel (a blend of Africans, Asians, Arabs, Latinos, and Europeans), Jews, and Judaism becomes harder to believe when it is obvious that Jews *are* people of color.

Increasing the numbers and visibility of racially and ethnically diverse Jews also helps to bridge the gaps with racial and ethnic groups. African American Jews are the best spokespeople to connect with other African Americans, Latino Jews can best speak to the Latino community, and so on. The more the Jewish community looks like America, the closer the Jewish community remains to all Americans. Because diverse Jews live in multiple cultures, they can serve to bridge communication gaps, cultural misunderstandings and shatter stereotypes.

Finally, the American Jewish community must support, encourage, and seek diversity, because **diversity has always been a vital part of Jewish history and heritage.** Throughout Jewish history, the Jewish people have borrowed from and added to other cultures wherever they were: Egypt or Ethiopia, Cartagena or Calcutta, Russia or Romania. The Jewish people have always grown by the addition of people from the surrounding cultures, changing and adapting with each influx of new ideas and different practices. Sometimes these expansions have been the result of the peaceful commingling of peoples living in close proximity to each other and other times the result of conquest and force. After all, even during the long sojourn of the Hebrews in Egypt, the Jewish slaves and their Egyptian masters

> *Diversity is such an important part of American identity, that the Jewish community would be well served by devoting resources and energy to racial and ethnic diversity within its own ranks.*

did not remain isolated from one another. No single ethnic or racial group has the "true Jew" credentials. Jews have survived by being a *people*, not a single race, and there is no better reason to embrace that tradition than the mere fact that it has always ensured group survival.

And so, in the pages that follow, we will explore ways to keep the Jewish community strong through building and maintaining a diverse population. To understand the current state of affairs, we examine the past, both inside the United States and, to a lesser extent, worldwide. We explore the history and experiences of ethnically and racially diverse Jews in the United States, in relation both to the American Jewish mainstream and to the minority communities to which they belong. We also examine policies and practices in the American Jewish community regarding conversion, adoption, intermarriage, and other areas that affect racially and ethnically diverse Jews. Finally, to help move the community toward the goal of a more diverse—and therefore stronger, more relevant—Jewish population, we make recommendations for change and examine how Be'chol Lashon (In Every Tongue), an initiative of the Institute for Jewish & Community Research to create a community inclusive of all Jews, regardless of race, ethnicity, or culture, can be a model for community-building around the world.

Describing the Tapestry

The term "Jews of color," defined by one website as "anyone who claim[s] heritages in addition to, or other than Ashkenazi,"[1] is hardly an adequate phrase to describe the innumerable ethnic and cultural backgrounds of the people who comprise the Jewish community today. And yet, we have no other terms or labels with which to replace it.

One sociological way of dividing the Jewish community by place of origin into three groups—Ashkenazi, Sephardi, and Mizrahi—denies the rich and varied cultural foundation of the contemporary American Jewish community. The same is true when one bifurcates "Jews of color" and "Ashkenazi Jews" into two distinct, monolithic groups. Just as Ashkenazi Jews are a mix of many peoples encountered during centuries of wandering throughout the Diaspora, Jews of color have different backgrounds, different life experiences, and different perspectives on their relationship to Judaism. These differences include geography, socio-economic class, ideology, culture, skin tone, language, paths to Judaism, and so on. What language, then, shall we use to describe multiracial and multi-ethnic Jews? What about those who are adopted from Asia by Ashkenazi parents? How would one categorize Indian Jews? Some African Americans whose families have been Jewish for over 100 years prefer to be known as "Hebrew Israelites," feeling that "Jew" refers to whites. Still other African American Jews have joined mainstream (read: Ashkenazi) synagogues. What about the *Anusim* (known also as Conversos or Crypto-Jews), whose ancestors were forced to convert to Catholicism in Spain and Portugal over 500 years ago?

How do we talk about ourselves when the language we have is too narrow and confining, like outdated racial categories on a census form? How do we describe a group for which there is no group label?

For the purposes of this book, we must use what is admittedly inadequate language: "Jews of color," "diverse Jews," "racially and ethnically diverse Jews." All of these terms refer to those who are in currently distinct subcultures from the majority Jewish community in the United States. Many people who fall into this category may not define themselves as "people of color," yet many in the mainstream view them as being "other." It is these individuals, whatever their origins and culture, whatever their skin tone, whatever their path to Judaism, that this book will discuss.

In the end, Jews of different cultures, languages, and colors are united by Torah, Hebrew, and Israel. With the cornerstones of Judaism as starting point, creating a community made up of all kinds of Jews is possible.

Racial and Religious Change in America

The borders that segment American society have always been more permeable than solid. Americans are a restless, creative people. We push boundaries, redefine culture, and reinvent ourselves as a matter of course. Our collective American self claims as fundamental the right to switch our addresses, change our names, shift our socioeconomic status, and even transform our very identities. We are a nation of immigrants and a country of endlessly peripatetic migrants. Between 1995 and 2000, more than 22 million people moved from one state to another.[1] Even the most seemingly fixed boundaries—race and ethnicity—have proven malleable in American society. Where once there existed violent divisions between European ethnic groups—"No Irish need apply," and so on—there remains for many European Americans only a romantic affiliation with their heritage, brought out on certain holidays and celebrated with others who may or may not share the same ancestry. Not everyone drinking green beer and wearing a shamrock on St. Patrick's Day is of Irish descent.

Official racial barriers have been slower to disintegrate. Until a 1967 Supreme Court decision declared them unconstitutional, laws against interracial marriage remained on the statutes of sixteen states, not all of them in the South. Another fourteen states had repealed them only shortly before that. (Of course, individuals had been defying both convention and the laws, by force or by choice, since the first Europeans arrived in North America.[2]) Still, racial segmentation, once so fearfully imposed, is no longer as obvious or enforceable, as more and more Americans cross racial divides not only in seeking romantic partners, but also in business, in housing, and in everyday relationships.

The trend toward an increasingly inter-ethnic and interracial American society is accelerating: the slowest growing population group in the United States is that of non-Hispanic whites. In some cities, like San Francisco and Los Angeles, no single ethnic or racial group constitutes more than 50% of the population, making it even more difficult for different groups to stay within their boundaries. As the cities go, so will the states. The inter-ethnic, interracial future of the United States is already being written. (Of course, certain cities, such as Chicago, remain largely segregated, and some American schools remain divided by race, but the barriers slowly continue to erode.)

That other great separator, religion, has also been losing its status as an absolute divide. The high fences that many organized religions once erected around their members have been trampled by the very people they were meant to enclose. With the entire landscape wide open to them, Americans increasingly think of religion as a spiritual journey on which they travel their own path to God, at best guided—but not dictated—by religious institutions. Building upon an old American tradition, many in the Baby Boomer generation have increasingly left rigid religious structures to become "spiritual seekers," preferring the term "Higher Power" and its concomitant Divine generalities to the term "God."[3] The third largest religiously identified group in America is now made up of those who have no religious identity, answering "none" or "other" when responding to polls.[4] (This includes Jews who retain a Jewish cultural identity but who say that they do not practice Judaism as a religion.) As the walls around strict religious affiliation come tumbling down, even those who choose to remain formally affiliated are switching religions at increasing rates, sometimes making multiple stops along their journey. Eighteen percent (18%) of the adult population of the United States now claim a different religion than the one in which they were raised.[5] Marriages between partners of different faiths are commonplace now, with children, if they are instructed in any religion, often being raised with cafeteria-style spirituality, allowing them to select those dishes that particularly appeal to them.

Jews are not immune to these changes. After all, Jews are Americans, integrated into nearly all aspects of American society. While more Jews live in urban and suburban areas of the Northeast than in any other region of the United States, Jews also live in every other part of the country, in small towns and rural areas, from Alaska to New Mexico, Hawaii to North Carolina. Jews occupy every socioeconomic stratum, are employed at all skill levels, and, increasingly, are indistinguishable from other Americans. Jews are not, as some people—both inside and outside the Jewish community—would like to believe, only one step away from the mythical 19th-century shtetl of *Fiddler on the Roof*. After all, Tevye and some of his children *did* come to America.

The high fences that many organized religions once erected around their members have been trampled by the very people they were meant to enclose.

Even some Jewish religious practices (although many would be loath to admit it) have been re-imagined to parallel mainstream—that is, Christian—America. Think Chanukah and its nightly gift exchange. Jewish religious identity is also changing in ways that parallel the American experience as a whole. In a 2000 study of the Jewish identity of "baby boomers" who belonged to a Jewish institution, Steve Cohen and Arnold Eisen found that the individuals they examined did not define themselves as Jews based primarily on religious belief, communal attachment through organizational affiliation, concern for Israel, or a broader concern about the Jewish people. Instead, like their fellow (non-Jewish) Americans, these people emphasized the individual and personal aspects of both their secular and religious lives.[6] In other words, they *chose* how to define their Jewish identities and what their relationship would be both to Jewish communal institutions and to Judaism. With religious identity being so individualistic (an inarguably American trait)[7], Jews can cross religious boundaries to meet their personal needs, just as non-Jews can cross into the Jewish community.

Given the changing ethnic and racial population of America, it is inevitable that more and more of those gentiles who venture into the Jewish community are not white.

And cross they do. Given the changing ethnic and racial population of America, it is inevitable that more and more of those gentiles who venture into the Jewish community are not white. Once they arrive, it may surprise them—and many white Jews—to find that they are not alone. While it is true that most American Jews are of Eastern and Central European descent, many are not, or at least not entirely. Jews around the world may identify themselves any number of ways: by cultural grouping, such as Ashkenazi, Sephardi, Mizrahi and Israelite; by geographic origin, such as European, African, Asian, Latino, Indian, and Caribbean; or by descent from one of the Tribes of Israel, as do the B'nei Menashe of India and the Lemba of southern Africa. Or, they may be a mix of several ethnic or racial groups. The Jewish community in the United States is no different. What once seemed a monolithic and homogeneous

Ashkenazi community (at least to Eastern and Central European Jews) is quickly becoming like so much of America: a living and evolving tradition, influenced not only by Ashkenazi and, to a lesser extent, Sephardic practices but also by innumerable racial, ethnic, and religious groups in America. While many of these changes are taking place because of external pressures—after all, an overwhelming majority of American Jews live and take part in a broader American culture more than they do in strictly Jewish milieus—a great deal of change is being wrought from within, by those diverse Jews whose history, experiences, behaviors, and attitudes we examine in this book. As with the country as a whole, the multi-ethnic, multiracial future of the American Jewish community is already unfolding.

Jewish Diversity in America and the Politics of Race

For the most part, ethnically and racially diverse Jews are invisible to the majority community *as Jews* even while they are sometimes very visible in their racial and ethnic differences. While some white Jews may be able to cite singular examples of diverse Jews in their own communities—the adopted Chinese daughter in one family, an African American convert in the synagogue, and so on—relatively few are aware of the sheer number and diversity of diverse Jews within the United States. For some white American Jews, the mere existence of other types of Jews can be somewhat surprising. While many people embrace both the idea and the reality of racially and ethnically diverse Jews, others may not. Benign ignorance, fear of the "stranger," and outright racism have led to hurtful encounters, isolation, and mutual distrust. In a diverse United States, this is not a specifically Jewish experience. American Jews must struggle within the constructs of racial politics that continue to encumber parts of American life today. Willingly or not, as part of American society, the Jewish community now finds itself navigating the racial landscape in America.

The racial divide is America's original sin, conceived in slavery and perpetuated through Jim Crow in the South, warfare with Native Americans, anti-Asian legislation in the West, and systematic discrimination throughout the rest of the United States. Most African American, Native American, Latino, and Asian families in America know, either directly or indirectly, the history of prejudice and discrimination in housing, in education, and, most starkly, in the justice system. Racial justice in America has vastly improved over the past two generations, and our civic norms now aggressively condemn discrimination. Still, anger, suspicion, and disrespect sometimes tarnish the relationship between the majority white population and other races. This legacy extends into the relationship between "majority" and "minority" Jews. Approaches for mitigating the effects of America's racial divide are beyond the scope of this book, yet it is impossible to examine the experiences of ethnically and racially diverse Jews without placing that discussion in its broader context. American Jews, whatever their race or ethnicity, are Americans, their lives circumscribed by the larger tensions of American life, including the history of racial politics in the United States.

For some white American Jews, the mere existence of other types of Jews can be somewhat surprising. While many people embrace both the idea and the reality of racially and ethnically diverse Jews, others may not.

To understand those politics, it is important first to examine how concepts of race, including definitions of "whiteness," have evolved since the earliest days of the United States and to see how Jews have fit into those concepts. Originally "race" meant "family," one's genetic line. Over time the concept changed to encompass divisions among peoples based on religion, culture, and, to some extent, skin tone. It was not until the 19th century that scientists constructed a definition that described a race as "a distinct biological group of human beings who were not all members of the same family but who shared inherited physical and cultural traits that were different from those shared within other races."[1] This biological definition of race was used as the justification for slavery and segregation of people of African descent. According to nineteenth-century racial theory, supported by supposedly empirical data, a racial hierarchy existed in which "the black race was always on the bottom and the white race on the top, with Asians and Indians in the middle."[2] People of mixed biological heritage clearly did not fit neatly into these definitions, and, since whiteness was the most desirable state, rules were created to define who was perceived as white and who was not. Prior to 1900, mixed black-white individuals with one-eighth or less African ancestry were deemed white and therefore eligible for access to privileges afforded their designated race. At the turn of the century, however, a "one-drop" law was instituted, which treated all people with even one black ancestor in their family history as black.[3]

Having no African ancestor, however, did not automatically qualify a person as white. Throughout most of American history, for people with no African heritage, biology was not the only—and not even necessarily the primary—determinant of an individual's racial status. Over the course of the 19th century, there were massive migrations of people to America from Ireland, Germany, Scandinavia, and Southern and Eastern Europe. Many of these groups were not initially accepted as white by the Anglo-Saxon population. Particularly singled out were Irish Catholics, who were described as "black," and Eastern European Jews, who were described as "foreign" and "Oriental." Jews were often depicted as having "kinky hair" and "thick lips," meant as negative stereotypical characterizations also used for Africans and African Americans. These designations were significant, because America's first naturalization law gave citizenship only to "free white persons." The designers of this law were Protestant and

Anglo-Saxon, and they meant to define "whiteness" as a reflection of themselves—and therefore to restrict access to the rights afforded citizens to others similar to them in both culture and appearance. With the large-scale immigration of Chinese and Japanese people to America in the early part of the 20th-century and the passage of the 1924 Immigration Act, which effectively choked off immigration from most Asian countries, "whiteness" was reconceived. Suddenly European immigrants of all sorts, including Italian Catholics and Eastern European Jews, were deemed "white," compared to Asian immigrants were legally declared "non-white."[4] In contrast to Northern and Western European Protestants, Jews were still considered "non-white" as recently as the 1950s, or later.

On the timeline of Jewish existence, the white status of Jews is relatively new.

On the timeline of Jewish existence, the white status of Jews is relatively new, a fact that surprises many contemporary Jews. As Lewis Gordon, Ph.D., Laura H. Carnell Professor of Philosophy at Temple University, asks, "How could there be, during a time when anti-miscegenation laws were in effect in the United States and parts of the Caribbean, these public marriages of European Jewish women and black men?" The answer, Professor Gordon points out, reveals "the complexity of Jewish identity in terms of how these communities [saw] Jews."[5] In other words, Jews were not "real" white people, or at least they were not white enough to violate the law when they married blacks. Karen Brodkin, author of *How Jews Became White Folks and What That Says about Race in America*, argues that the critical step in the transformation of Jews from non-white to white came after World War II, when legislative changes, especially the GI Bill of Rights and federal suburban home loan policy, gave Jews opportunities—economic, educational, professional, residential, and so on—that had previously been more available to people who were Protestant, sometimes Catholic, and always white.[6] Many Jews used these newly given privileges to move beyond the legally and popularly condoned anti-Semitism that forced Jews to have limited economic status and neighborhood choice. Jews of European descent began to rapidly join the ranks of the social and economic middle class in the United States, albeit very slowly at first and with resistance from the Protestant establishment.[7]

In being given these opportunities, these newly "white" Jews were separated from African Americans and other racial minorities, including other minority Jews. Whiteness became—and remains—the norm for the majority of American Jews. Beginning in the 1950s and 1960s, however, many Jews found that being white was a *situational* rather than an *absolute* status. In interacting with non-Jewish America, Jews were aware that they were not universally white, when "white" meant free of restrictions to move about society. In the face of anti-Semitism, too, Jews were aware of their status as "other," especially when other white people were the perpetrators. As they related to people of color, including Jews of color, however, mainstream Jews *experienced* the privileges of being white. They could pass as part of the majority, even if they sometimes *felt* otherwise and could empathize with other minority groups. They also experienced anti-Semitism as a reflection of their whiteness: for example, Jews became the primo representation of whiteness to blacks.

Over time, the fact that Jews were increasingly considered white by others and saw themselves as white raised considerable anxiety within the Jewish community. By becoming white, were Jews giving up their Jewish identities? Had they become "too white"? The rising concern about the intermarriage rate reflected this question. In 1957, 3.5% of Jews were marrying non-Jews.[8] By the 1990, almost 50% of Jews were marrying non-Jews. Their white status was a reflection of the assimilation Jews so avidly sought, yet it consequently created a different set of concerns and fears within the Jewish community about group survival and "too much" assimilation. In the early 1900s, Jewish community centers were originally created to assimilate newly arrived immigrants, to help them to be more "American." Now, generations later, Jewish community centers are called upon to help fully assimilated Jewish Americans to become more knowledgeable and involved Jews. Shedding old world identities has given way to helping to preserve a distinct Jewish identity.

Over and over, rabbis and other Jewish leaders cite the high level of interreligious marriage between Jews and non-Jews. To combat this trend, the Jewish community has invested heavily in Jewish day schools, established continuity commissions, and reaffirmed the need for endogamous marriage.[9] This level of intermarriage, which began to rise in the 1960s, is seen by many to be a great tragedy. For some rabbis, the damage to the Jewish people created by intermarriage is greater than the conflict in the Middle East and anti-Semitism, and is on par with the Holocaust.[10]

Jews seek to be white, but not too white.

Some scholars argue that intermarriage is considered a threat to the Jewish community because there is a fear that the children of intermarriage will not be Jewish and that, even if the children are raised as Jews, the strength of the Jewishness of the members of the household (in terms of religious observance, communal participation, and ethnic identity) will be diluted.[11] There is a debate in the Jewish community on how to face this threat. On the one hand, there are those such as Rabbis Harold Schulweis and Edward Feinstein[12] who call for a more inclusive community, while others, like Steven Bayme, say that the Jewish community should focus on the "core," Jews who are most traditional in terms of religious practice and organizational affiliation.[13]

The Conservative and Orthodox movements have tended to emphasize the renewal of commitment and tradition. In 1991, for example, the Conservative movement's United Synagogue Youth (USY) urged its members to refrain from dating non-Jews and prevented anyone doing so from becoming an officer.[14] However, in 2001 an arm of Conservative Judaism, the Federation of Jewish Men's Clubs, published a book entitled, *Building the Faith: A Book of Inclusion for Duel-Faith Families* by Rabbi Charles Simon[15], that calls for the movement to increase the involvement of intermarried families in Jewish communal life. It is written for congregational rabbis and lay leaders, advocating for increased participation of non-Jews in synagogue life even while upholding the movement's prohibitions against religious intermarriage, rabbinical officiation at mixed-marriage ceremonies and non-Jewish participation in certain rituals in the synagogue.

There are specific efforts aimed at "in-reach," encouraging Jews who are unaffiliated or marginally affiliated to become more involved in Jewish life, such as Rabbi Ephraim Buchwald's National Jewish Outreach Program.

> The National Jewish Outreach Program was founded in 1987 in response to the urgent need to prevent the loss of Jews to Jewish life due to assimilation and lack of Jewish knowledge.... [It] reaches out to Jews by offering them positive, joyous, Jewish educational opportunities and experiences.[16]

Chabad-Lubavitch, a philosophy, a movement, and an organization, has become quite adept in helping Jews reconnect to their Judaism, with dedicated and passionate rabbis and programs all over the world. "Today 4,000 full-time emissary families apply 250-year-old principles and philosophy to direct more than 3,300 institutions (and a workforce that numbers in the tens of thousands) dedicated to the welfare of the Jewish people worldwide."[17]

Like Rabbi Buchwald's efforts, the focus is on in-reach, motivating born Jews to embrace their Judaism.

Other efforts are aimed at reaching out to the non-Jewish spouses of mixed-married couples and welcoming potential converts. The Union for Reform Judaism (URJ, formerly the Union of American Hebrew Congregations, or UAHC), the national organization of the Reform movement, has made a particular commitment to outreach (although the financial support has been minimal and was severely cut in 2003) by inviting "Jewish choices for all — Jews and non-Jews, young and old, interfaith and Jewish families."[18] The Reform movement sponsors introduction to Judaism classes entitled, "A Taste of Judaism: Are you Curious?" with the goal of "providing welcoming and meaningful Jewish experiences in a rich, engaging Jewish community." Established by Ash and Gloria Gerecht in 1995, the National Center to Encourage Judaism provides matching grants to congregations that advertise "Introduction to Judaism" and "Taste of Judaism" in the secular press. Additionally, the Gerecht Family Institute for Outreach provides comprehensive outreach education for students at Hebrew Union College-Jewish Institute on Religion (HUC-JIR).[19] Other independent organizations, such as the Jewish Outreach Institute founded by the late Egon Mayer, Ph.D., "empowers and helps the Jewish community welcome and fully embrace all members of interfaith families into Jewish life."[20]

Broader mainstream Jewish communal efforts aimed at encouraging Jews to marry other Jews rely on building a stronger Jewish identity and have included free trips to Israel, and incentives to send children to Jewish day schools and summer camps. Indeed, the emphasis on Jewish education as a preventative of a religiously mixed marriage has become an almost sacrosanct truth of the Jewish communal structure, whether true or not.

Still, all of these efforts are rooted in the desire to be religiously distinct, but not marginalized. Jews seek to be white, but not too white.

The Last Taboo: Interracial Marriage

For the past three and a half decades, one of the great social taboos of American society has been breaking down at a more rapid rate than in the past: interracial marriage is becoming more normative. Jews have been part of that change. In the Institute for Jewish & Community Research's study of diverse Jews, nearly half the marriages or partnerships were between people of different races. This does not indicate a new phenomenon in American society. One has only to look at the skin tones of Americans to confirm that interracial relationships have always existed, some by choice and some the forced, unwelcome unions during slavery. For years, people who chose to enter into interracial relationships had to navigate through social and legal condemnation. Since the 1960s, as those barriers have been weakening, the number of children born of interracial unions has been increasing, and that change has led to a growing number of multiracial Jewish children.

Navigating prejudice, on the one hand, and moving among multiple identities, on the other hand, are most manifest around the question of marriage and partners. How does one find the right fit between race and religion when choosing a mate? Does an

African American Jew marry someone who is Jewish but not
black, or black but not Jewish, or only another African American
Jew? Which is the trump card—religion or race? As Rabbi Capers
Funnye, the African American spiritual leader of Beth Shalom
B'nai Zaken Ethiopian Hebrew Congregation in Chicago, asks,
"Would you rather see your daughters and sons marry someone
who looks like me or the whitest gentile?"

The concern about finding a suitable partner was voiced
frequently among the diverse Jews in the Institute study. Michael,
a 35-year-old black Orthodox Jew, complained about "the difficulties and exclusion in the marriage partnering process" that he
experienced. His worry about finding a spouse is shared by many
racially and ethnically diverse Jews, for whom marrying another
Jew is very important. Those who can not see beyond the taboo of
interracial marriage see no future
for non-whites in America to
become Jews. While she was still in
the process of converting, Roxanne,
a young, single black woman was
told, "Too bad there is no one for
you to marry."

*"Would you rather see
your daughters and sons
marry the blackest Jew or
the whitest gentile?"*

The Institute for Jewish & Community Research survey asked
three questions about marriage: between a white Jew and an
African American Jew; between a white Jew and a Latino Jew; and
between a white Jew and an Asian Jew. A mere 17% of the respondents believed that most white Jews would be comfortable with
their child marrying an African American Jew. (Only 2%
"strongly" agreed.) For Latinos and Asians, the numbers were
significantly higher: 51% agreed that most white Jews would be
comfortable with their child marrying either a Latino Jew or an
Asian Jew. (See Figure 3.) The long racial divide in America
between blacks and whites is most evident in this part of the
study, where race trumps religion in determining eligible romantic

partners. (Just as some potential parents decline to adopt a child of a race different from their own for fear that a transracial adoption will be hard on the child, some people worry about having a family with someone of a different race because they believe mixed-race children may encounter similar challenges.)

Diverse Jews believe that black Jews would be more comfortable than white Jews with the idea of black/white Jewish marriages (59%). With only 17% of the respondents believing that most white Jews would be comfortable with their child marrying a black Jew, even an observant black Jew, it is all too clear that diverse Jews might feel deeply rejected by the mainstream Jewish community, cut off from their own future and the future their children might have there. (See Figure 4.)

Ruth, who was born in New York in 1935 of a white Jewish mother and a black non-practicing Anglican father, was initially raised with no religious practices, because as soon as her parents married, her grandparents "sat *shiva* [for Ruth's mother]. They disowned her. She was no longer part of the family. And when she became disowned, she disowned her own Jewishness. And she

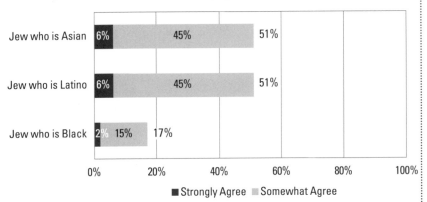

Figure 3
Attitudes about interracial marriage among Jews (Percent agreeing)
To what extent do you agree with the statement, "Most white Jews would be comfortable with their child marrying a ..."

Source: Survey of Racially & Ethnically Diverse Jews in the United States, Institute for Jewish & Community Research, 2001.

insisted that my father do the same [with his religion]." Until high school, Ruth attended all-black schools, where she noticed other children celebrating Easter and Christmas. "I started asking about different people, why they were celebrating and we were cele-brating nothing. So [my mother] decided she was going to intro-duce me to what Judaism was about." Ruth's mother approached a Reform congregation near their house in Brooklyn and "told them she would like to come in with her daughter, and that she hadn't been involved in her faith and would like to get started again. [The rabbi] welcomed her with open arms ... until he saw me. So when *we* went in, *we* were escorted out. Physically escorted out of the synagogue by the scruff of our necks."

The black side of her family was no more welcoming. Although she lived in an all-black segregated neighborhood, she thought of herself "as Jewish, because I didn't want to be what my father was, because when my father married my mother, my father's family disowned her and me." Ruth was left with no solid identity. She never returned to formal Jewish religious practice.

Figure 4
Attitudes about marriage between black and white Jews
(Percent agreeing)

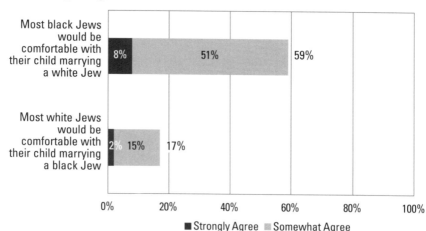

Source: *Survey of Racially & Ethnically Diverse Jews in the United States, Institute for Jewish & Community Research, 2001.*

Now that both of her parents are dead, Ruth continues to waver in her identity. "Sometimes I'm Jewish; sometimes I'm black. I'm whatever."[1]

In race-conscious America, conceiving a child with someone of another race has been an inherently political act. While any interracial union carries with it a set of stereotypes, prejudices, and assumptions that accompanies the children for the rest of their lives, a black and white mixed-race couple evokes the strongest and most ancient of reactions within the American psyche. It is perhaps inevitable, then, that in the United States, where racial and ethnic communities demand allegiance and where people of mixed heritage find themselves suspect everywhere, that many multiracial people become deeply involved in the politics of race and identity in America. It is both a personal and a public search for an answer to the question, "Who am I?" and a fitting legacy of their parents' initial political act. Yet, these norms are changing. As more and more Americans acknowledge their mixed identities (rather than pretending they do not exist), crossing racial boundaries is becoming less political. Indeed, increasingly our popular culture sees multiculturalism as ordinary, not suspect at all. Over time, having more than one identity is becoming a plus, not a liability. In her book, *Black, Jewish and Interracial,* Katya Gibel Azoulay asserts that "there might be more likelihood that a Jewish child in an interracial marriage would be more sensitive to [...] the disjuncture between people's stereotyped equation of Jews having white skin and the true variation that exists."[2]

Multiracial individuals face the challenging task of sorting through multiple identities as they try to figure out where they fit

> *Increasingly our popular culture sees multiculturalism as ordinary, even desirable. Over time, having more than one identity is becoming a plus, not a liability.*

in. Sasha, whose multiracial, multi-ethnic background sent her on a journey through many ethnic-based organizations on her college campus, finally settled with the Intertribal Student Union because everyone in the club was mixed. For other multiracial Jews, the journey is ongoing.

Feet in Many Rivers: Navigating Multiple Identities

The questions of blood, genes, and looking Jewish can create conflict and confusion for many racially and ethnically diverse Jews as they attempt to balance their multiple identities. Since the Jewish community is largely unaware of the existence of diverse Jews, it is often easier for a diverse Jew to identify culturally with his or her race than with the mainstream Jewish community. At the same time, they may feel discrimination from their racial group for their identification with Judaism. The result is a bifurcation of identities, having feet in many rivers, swimming freely in none.

During a discussion of their identities as Jews, Danielle and Leland found themselves at odds over how to reconcile their black and Jewish identities. Leland described becoming a Jew as a "a restatement of who I really am." He identified with Julius Lester, who, in his autobiography, *Lovesong: Becoming a Jew*, said that when he looked in a mirror, he didn't see a black face but rather who he really was.[1] Leland said that he had a similar experience since his conversion. "When I look at myself in the mirror," he said, "I am Yisrael now. I know who I am. This is the name by which God calls me."

Danielle responded, "I don't feel like I have to renounce my blackness [...] to embrace [my Jewish self]."

Leland explained that he was not renouncing his blackness; rather, he was recognizing that seeing himself only as black was hiding from his true self. He wondered whether he would have had the same struggle with his identity had he been white.

The way in which diverse Jews struggle to reconcile their Jewish religious identity with their racial or cultural identity seems to depend, in part, on the individual's path to Judaism. Those who converted to Judaism tend to feel a sense of completeness, of joy, at having found their way to Jewish religious practice. Religious fervor carries them through the struggle, and they are sure of who they are, since they have had to undertake an arduous journey to claim that part of their identity.

> *"I feel very strongly black-identified and very strongly Jewish-identified and am rejected often in both settings."*

For biracial people who have one Jewish parent, the question of "Jewish blood" influences their sense of themselves. As with other "born" Jews, biracial Jews do not necessarily feel the need to pursue a strong religious identity in order to maintain their connection to being Jewish. Kim, a 23-year-old woman, separates being "culturally Jewish" from the religion of Judaism. In addition, she stakes her claim to a Jewish identity based on blood. "I don't identify as being culturally Jewish, though I certainly identify with it through [the religion of] Judaism and somewhat on a racial level, given that I have a Jewish mother. I do, however, identify as being culturally Japanese and again somewhat on a racial level because my father is Japanese."

Younger biracial Jews have the advantage of coming of age during a time when there are more and more individuals with similar backgrounds, but that does not mean that they all have an easy time finding their place in a world that often insists on singular allegiances. Andrea is the daughter of a white Jewish father and black non-Jewish mother. She grew up with a strong Jewish identity. "I found that it was an issue for black people that I was not black-identified," she says. "When I went to college, I was asked to choose essentially. I had an experience at an orientation [at a West Coast law school] where there were people talking about the services available to students of color. I finally said, 'You know, this sounds great. Most of the students in this environment are white. Can you talk about the interaction between the students of color and the white students?' And there was silence. Finally, this one black student said, 'This is a very tough place. It is best if you stick to your own kind.'" But what is her "kind"? Where do people with multiple backgrounds fit in? As she stood at the orientation, Andrea answered the question herself: "And I thought, 'So this is the universe of half black, half Jewish bisexuals from New York.'"

Although she felt singular in that moment, Andrea is not alone in her half-and-half experience as a multiracial person. In her review of *The Autograph Man*, Susan Katz Miller, herself the child of an interfaith couple, can identify with novelist Zadie Smith's insights on dual identity and possible ambivalence towards Judaism:

> Smith tells us that Alex's "instinct was to detest grouping of all kinds—social, racial, national or political; he had never joined so much as a swimming club." Many intercultural children, whether we are interfaith or mixed race, will recognize this allergy to grouping (especially when we cannot choose our own group) and to clubs (which by definition exclude).[2]

Christine, whose mother is white and Jewish and whose father is black and Protestant, says, "I feel very strongly black-identified and very strongly Jewish-identified and am rejected often in both settings, so it's difficult." For Christine and Andrea, as for many other multiracial respondents in our study, the challenge is both internal and external. Who do they know themselves to be? Who does the world see when it looks at them?

Diana, a 32-year-old biracial woman raised by her white Jewish mother, brushes aside other people's need for her to declare her identity. "The world really requires you to make a decision about your identity and stick to one. That is much more convenient for the rest of the world." She believes that having multiple identities is part of being human. All people have different identities, she says, "because they're different people when they're at work or when they're with their families or when they're with friends or just men or just women. As diverse an identity as most interracial people have. It's just more obvious. It's just more on the surface." In her struggle to understand her many selves, she has discovered that she doesn't need to settle on any one of them. "I fully embrace my schizophrenic identities. I think it's really healthy to have a fluid sense of identity. And to allow that to be okay. Because I don't think that I've really exhausted the efforts to come to one singular, integrated identity that I am all the time. That just has never happened."

> For many multiracial respondents, the challenge is both internal and external. Who do they know themselves to be? Who does the world see when it looks at them?

Kimani, who was born in the late 1960s, found that her white Jewish mother encouraged her awareness of racial politics. "Ever since I was very young, Mom has been pro-black. It's a weird situation; she hates being white. She hasn't become black—she can't. [But] she does not like the white race. So she was basically the black influence. My [black Jamaican non-Jewish] dad was the more white one in the family. What was taught to him in Jamaica was 'the lighter, the better.' [My mom] is a very angry person and just hates the injustices of what whites have done and still do to blacks, and [she] just hates being part of that race because of that." She encouraged Kimani and her brother to develop strong identities as black people. "Most people don't think I'm biracial. They can't tell. So Mom was very honest and said, 'This is what society is like. Don't be sucked in. Be strong. You're a black woman. You'll be seen as a black woman.'" Despite her encouragement of her daughter to assume a racial identity based on what society *sees* her to be, Kimani's mother "will take on this black persona. She fools people all the time. To me she doesn't look black, but she has the attitude." Kimani finds her mother's assumed blackness upsetting and thinks of it as a false identity. "I don't like the way my mom behaves with people because it's not what she is. It's one thing if you *are* black and you switch in and out of a black vernacular or whatever you'd want to call it. Mom isn't,

> *"I grew up a regular little Jewish colored girl."*

and it would get on my nerves when she would do that, because it's not really her. It's just false pretenses, and I don't like that."

With her parents having seemingly switched racial identities, Kimani was left without a solid identity of her own. "When I'm around Jewish people, I love to shock them and say, 'Yes, I'm Jewish.' And at times I get this overwhelming feeling of how lucky I am to have come from such diverse cultures. I can really say that *this* is me and *this* is me. But because I haven't really delved deeply into each one, I'm not really a part of it, and that's where I think I'm losing. I wish I had grabbed onto one—actually I wish I had grabbed onto both—but I took the superficial aspects of both. I think that's partly because of my mom and dad. I get angry at them a lot for that, because I wish they had directed me. What I've come to on my own, I guess, is being a black feminist. Very much what I've studied and learned has been male-oriented, and now I'm becoming more women-oriented. It's been refreshing. It's like I have a voice, too."[3]

Politics—racial, gender, sexual—is always (and sometimes only) about the desire to have a voice, a recognized and recognizable identity. The voice of a Jew is already multifarious, modified by movement affiliation, marriage, and religious practices, among other influences. Racial and ethnic diversity add other notes and timbres creating, at its best, a chord. To arrive at that harmonious sound—and to have it be heard—requires both commitment and strength. For some mixed-race Jews, the process of creating harmony can be exhausting. For others, it is all they know. Sandy, who is in her mid-fifties, is the daughter of a Jewish Ukrainian mother and a black-identified father, himself the son of a Cuban-Chinese father and black mother. Her father was a Communist, her mother a politically active progressive. Sandy works in politics herself and has forged her own identity— her own voice—out of the many notes available to her. According to Sandy, creating one's own voice is a particularly Jewish trait. "I was born [in New York], and I say I grew up a regular little Jewish colored girl. I think of myself as being Jewish, not white. I don't think of Jews as being white because they're Semites—they don't come from Europe, even though they come from Europe—no more than you would think of an Arab as being white. I know they spent several hundred years in Europe, but Jews can self-identify. To me, Jewishness is not just a religion, it's a culture, and I come from that part of the culture that was oppressed, that connected its oppression with the oppression of everyone else, that developed an ethos and a theory around what it meant to be thrown out and dispossessed in the world. That's what it means to me to be Jewish. I know that there

> "To me, Jewishness is not just a religion, it's a culture, and I come from that part of the culture that was oppressed."

are other ways that other people have of being Jewish, but that's not my way."

Unlike some of the younger multiracial people who felt they had to be Jewish in some contexts, black in another, Latino in a third, and so on, Sandy's response to the world's demanding that she choose her place is to choose them all. "I had a therapist that once called me counterphobic, which means that instead of running away, I go towards what I fear. I hide in the open. I bring my whole life wherever I go. So I will tell people I'm black and Cuban, Chinese and Jewish. I will say that no matter where I am. To some extent, that insulates me." When she was younger, Sandy went along with attempts to force her towards a singular identity, marrying a black man. "I was stupid," she says. "And now I have stepped over the boundaries. I'm not sure I ever lived within those boundaries to begin with. I've always lived in another kind of world and always created a milieu for myself that was truly multiracial. It's just this place, this clearing that you make in your life, that whoever's around you loves you and whatever you do, it's okay. As you get older, you make that space, you have some armor against the slings and arrows of people who don't know you and who are going to make judgments about your life that they don't know [anything] about."[4] Sandy, in the way of many diverse Jews faced with having to choose among multiple identities, has become her own kind of Jew, her own kind of person of color, her own kind of woman. And in doing so, she has taken her place in the larger community of diverse Jews.

The question of appearances (i.e., looking Jewish or not) is difficult to resolve for many mixed-race people. For Jess, reconciling her two cultures is not a challenge, but she attributes her ease, in part, to her skin color and how her color facilitates the ability of each community to claim her. "I was raised with both [identities], and I wish that I had been raised with more of both. I have no sense of confusion whatsoever. There are many people who describe me as half-Jewish and half-Latin or half-Peruvian. And I feel like I'm all of both. But it is exhausting. I know this year I had a *challah* baking workshop for Rosh Hashonah, where I showed people how to bake three-pound loaves of challah. We made 80 pounds of challah together. It took hours and hours. And then, I built a sukkah, and, of course, we had a lot of mangoes and other Latin food hanging in there. And then I also built an altar for *Día de los Muertos* [Day of the Dead]. So I'm exhausted, but I feel like I'm participating fully in both sides of my culture and integrating it. But there is a lot of pressure to just go one way, and [that depends on] what our appearance is. Because I know other people I've talked to who are darker-skinned or much lighter-skinned. It is easier for them to go one way or the other, or they have a lot more pressure or face a lot more racism or anti-Semitism in having to pick. And I think because of what I look like, I get to choose more easily than other people may be able to."

> It is not uncommon for diverse Jews to face prejudice from within their racial or ethnic group.

As Jess and others point out, appearance influences how a diverse Jew is received within the Jewish community. The opposite is true within racial communities. There, unless one is wearing Jewish religious garb or symbols, appearance is not a marker of one's other identity. The ability to "pass" as a non-Jew creates additional conflicts of identity for diverse Jews, sometimes even a denial of their Jewish identity. As a result, it is not uncommon for diverse Jews to face prejudice from within their racial or ethnic group. Nearly half (44%) of the survey respondents reported sometimes (36%) or often (8%) experiencing anti-Jewish attitudes in their ethnic or racial communities. (See Figure 5.)

Anne, a black woman, has heard anti-Semitic comments from other African Americans. "I have been in situations in which people have said something about 'Jews controlling everything.' I said something back about stereotypes, etc., but was not as vehement as I should have been. I did not volunteer my own spiritual/religious leanings."

Some African American Jews have a particularly problematic relationship with their racial communities, reflecting the larger politics of race in America. On questions involving the Israeli/Palestinian conflict, some African Americans, both Jewish and non-Jewish, may tend to identify with Palestinians, for example, and see Israelis—and by extension Jews—as the oppressors. Pro-Israel African American Jews may suffer derision from other black people. Michelle, who is black, found herself the target of another African American's anti-Israel campaign at work. "[He] would cut out anti-Israel articles from the newspaper and place them on my desk at work. He would also place clippings with Louis Farrakhan quotes on my desk first thing in the morning. This went on for several months until I told him to stop. He stopped the clippings, but he gave new black employees the

Figure 5
How often have you or your family experienced anti-Jewish attitudes in your ethnic or racial community?

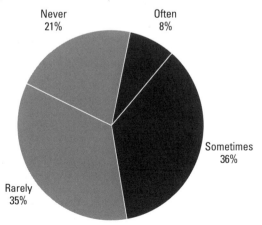

Source: Survey of Racially & Ethnically Diverse Jews in the United States, Institute for Jewish & Community Research, 2001.

tour by my office so they could see what a black Zionist looks like."

When a diverse Jew has no visible markings of religious affiliation, the decision to "come out" as a Jew can require valor. It may also evoke some particularly disheartening responses from non-Jewish members of racial communities. Rachel was "a member of a black women's chat room, where I thought we were all 'free' to discuss any issue. When I said I was a Jew, one woman, with an 'Africanized' name, said she hated all Jews and I could kiss her ass. Since no one spoke out against her prejudice, they obviously condoned it. I unsubscribed. Those of us who have experienced racism don't hesitate to inflict it on others. But this makes me stronger and more determined not to do this to others, especially Muslims."

When a diverse Jew has no visible markings of religious affiliation, the decision to "come out" as a Jew can require valor.

Many Latino Jews have to navigate through assumptions on the part of other Latinos that they are Catholic. They also struggle against institutional dissemination of anti-Semitic rhetoric. Linda, a 19-year-old whose father is white Ashkenazi, suffered during visits with her mother's Catholic family in Colombia. "As I was growing up, my Catholic Colombian relatives genuinely believed that Jews were evil because they were the ones who had Jesus Christ killed. It is saddening and disturbing to hear these messages of hate directed at your community by another one of your communities, especially when your own family is saying these barbarous words as you are growing up."

Rabbi Rigoberto Emmanuel ("Manny") Viñas, the Cuban American Orthodox rabbi of the Lincoln Park Jewish Center in Yonkers, New York, and founder and director of El Centro de Estudios Judíos "Torat Emet," found that his becoming Jewish raised the suspicion among other people of color that he was trying to leave their ranks. They, like some diverse Jews themselves, equated being Jewish with being white. Rabbi Viñas has found that "most of the discrimination I experience comes at the hands of black and Latino people in New York. That usually takes the form of [questions like], 'Who do you think you are? Don't you know that you'll always be a spic? Do you think you're white? Do you think that by becoming Jewish you're better than me?' They say anti-Semitic things. [Then they say], 'I don't mean you. I mean everyone else.' But I know that they mean me."[5]

The rejection and distrust that many diverse Jews must contend with inside both their racial communities and the Jewish community is a logical but not immutable result of their invisibility. People of color may not know that there are Jews who look like them, with a similar cultural and social background; most mainstream Jews do not know of the existence of other types of Jews. It is not surprising that rejection could run both ways.

The problem becomes self-perpetuating when racially and ethnically diverse Jews do not interact with the white majority or with each other. How can racial communities understand that there are Jews among them—Jews who desire to remain affiliated with their racial communities—if the Jews themselves remain silent? And, while some diverse Jews find homes in synagogues and Jewish organizations and feel part of the majority community, others may never have seen another diverse Jew. Visual reinforcement is crucial in building a healthy sense of identity, of feeling that one is not alone in the world. Visible role models are especially important, particularly in leadership positions. Of course, all kinds of Jews are detached from Jewish communal life. They do not belong to synagogues; they do not contribute to Jewish philanthropies, and so on. Many diverse Jews are even more alienated. Diverse Jews often feel alone, isolated and unwelcome. They remain stuck in the swirling waters, unsure where to take the next step.

Jews Have Always Been Diverse

The North American Jewish experience is built upon foundations of diversity as old as the Jewish people, a fact that may have been lost in the consciousness of some American Jews. The historical home of the Jews lies at the geographic crossroads of Africa, Asia, and Europe. Jews are an amalgam of many peoples, and Jewish origins include a multitude of languages, tribes, and skin colors.

The essence of the story of the Jewish people is based on the Exodus from Egypt, where Jews sojourned for 400 years. The Exodus story is not only a metaphor for the escape from slavery to freedom; it is also a geographic journey that took the Hebrew people across the Sinai from Asia to Africa and back again. Over time, ancient Judea, Samaria, Israel, and Canaan were conquered by the Greeks, Romans, and Turks, among others, and the Hebrews had long and deep connections with other Mediterranean and European cultures.

The story of the Jewish people is filled with interracial and intercultural mixing. After all, Israel's greatest prophet, Moses, married Zipporah, an Ethiopian. Solomon and David each took wives from Africa. Joseph married an Egyptian—an African. For much of Jewish history, there was not a matzah ball in sight. While so much of contemporary Jewish consciousness comes from Eastern and Central Europe and—to a lesser extent, the Iberian Peninsula—Jews have deep roots in Africa. Even at their beginning, Jews were a blend of different groups. As Ephraim Isaac, Ph.D., the Ethiopian-born director of the Institute of Semitic Studies in Princeton, New Jersey, explains:

> Over two thousand years ago, the Jews were an ethnic group—but even then not a "perfect" one. Since then, Jews have intermingled with many nations and absorbed many proselytes. [...] The ancient Israelites were not a racial unit but a sacral association, called an amphictyony by some scholars. They were a people bound together by a common language, and common territory, similar historical experience, and common consciousness. The Ark of the Covenant was the main sacred cult object and formed the center of worship. They had a primary unit of social and territorial organiza-tion, [...]and extended family that was then patrilineal. [...] It is the centrality of concern for the Torah revealed on Mount Sinai and the great values of our heritage that bind us together as Jews.[1]

The historical home of the Jews lies at the geographic crossroads of Africa, Asia, and Europe.

From their original homes in Africa and Asia, Jews spread throughout the globe. The World Jewish Congress survey of the Jewish Diaspora indicated that as of the mid-16th century, Jewish communities could be found in countries as far-flung as Jamaica, Brazil, Yemen, Afghanistan, Ethiopia, India, and China, as well as in many countries in Europe. Even today, the World Jewish Congress identifies 120 countries with a Jewish community. Jewish communities can be found on every continent on earth (Antarctica excluded).[2]

That snapshot of the worldwide geographic distribution of Jews is dramatically different from what it was prior to World War II. Before the Holocaust, Europe was the center of the world's Jewish population, with relatively large populations also spread throughout North America, North Africa, and the Middle East. After much of European Jewry was murdered, most Jews living in Muslim countries were forcibly expelled and migrated to Israel, resulting in two major population centers: the United States, with a population of over six million Jews,[3] and Israel, with 5.3 million Jews.[4]

The Jews that live in the other 118 countries are as varied as the countries themselves. There are immigrant communities that may look different from the surrounding populations in which they find themselves, as well as Jews who are, at first glance, hard to distinguish from the larger communities in which they live. Just as is happening in the United States today, from their earliest days Jews around the world married local people, and, as a result, they came to resemble the people around them. Still, they retained their Jewish identities and religious observances, only they did so with a local accent and flavor.

> The story of the Jewish people is filled with interracial mixing.

As would be expected, the cuisine of these diverse Jews reflects the regions in which they live. According to the *Book of Jewish Food* by Claudia Roden, an Egyptian Jew who lives in London:

> Jewish food tells the story of an uprooted, migrating people.[…] There is really no such thing as Jewish food. […] Local regional food becomes Jewish when it travels with Jews to new homelands. […] The main influence on the development and shaping of their cuisine was their mobility. […] Jews moved to escape persecution or

economic hardship, or for trade. […] The vehicles of gastronomic knowledge were merchants and peddlers, traveling rabbis, preachers and teachers, students and cantors, professional letter carriers, beggars (who were legion), and pilgrims on their way to and from the Holy Land. […] It is possible, by examining family dishes, to define the identity and geographical origin of a family line.[5]

For example, Ethiopian Jews, like non-Jewish Ethiopians, eat their food with *injera*, a flat, spongy bread used to scoop up purées of lentils, vegetables, and other spicy stews. In the south of India, the Jews of Cochin make curries with chilies and coconut, ingredients not found in typical Ashkenazi kitchens.[6] None of this should be a surprise, since Ashkenazi cooking reflects its Eastern and Central European origins as well. One would no more expect Ashkenazi Jews to stuff kreplach with tamarind paste than to think that Indian Jews might use schmaltz in a fish curry.

> *While Asian, African, and Latin American Jews are racially and ethnically different from European Jews, they wear* kippot *and* tallitot, *read Hebrew and chant Torah.*

The similarities between these communities and the majority Jewish community, however, are as significant as the differences. While Asian, African, and Latin American Jews are racially and ethnically different from European Jews, they wear *kippot* and *tallitot*, read Hebrew and chant Torah. They hold Shabbat services, have rabbis as their spiritual leaders, and say the blessings over the bread and wine on Shabbat. They have synagogues and *mikvot*. Many Jews may look different from their fellow Jews of European origin, but they pray to the same God and consider themselves part of the same people. Jews are diverse, yet they are tied to each other historically and religiously.

Most Jews are aware of the historic, geographic, and cultural diversity of the Jewish people—to a degree. The majority of American Jews identify as Ashkenazi, those who came from Roman lands after the destruction of the Second Temple, settling in Western and Central Europe. However, even the great variety of European cultures from which most American Jews descended is understood only in a cursory way. Few realize how complex and varied the communities were from place to place, the distinct nature of Hungarian Jews as opposed to Polish Jews or Greek Jews. Most know a little something about Sephardic Jews, who traditionally spoke Ladino, a Judeo-Spanish dialect, not Yiddish. Much less is known about Mizrahi Jews (Jews of the Arab world) and the rich societies that once thrived in Yemen, Iran, or Iraq. Relatively few people know about the ancient communities of Jews in India, despite Jews having lived there for centuries. Another little known story is that of the African Jewish Diaspora, which has received relatively little scholarly attention.

The following is a brief overview of some traditional, often lesser known Jewish communities. Additionally, there are examples of newer communities of Jews, as well as emerging communities in transition to Judaism. They illustrate the scope and variety of diversity of Jews around the world. In aggregate, the potential for the growth of the Jewish people in this vast array of communities is promising.

Sephardic Jews

Although some Sephardic Jews do not necessarily consider themselves "Jews of color," they are included in this study of ethnically and racially diverse Jews because they are part of distinct cultural heritage different from the majority Ashkenazi population in the United States, Israel, and elsewhere.

The reconquest of Spain and its reunification under Isabel and Fernando in 1492 resulted in the expulsion of the entire Jewish community of 200,000 from Spain. "Tens of thousands of refugees died while trying to reach safety. [...] The Jews' expulsion had been the pet project of the Spanish Inquisition, headed by Father Tomás de Torquemada. Torquemada believed that as long as the Jews remained in Spain, they would influence the tens of thousands of recent Jewish [forced] converts to Christianity to continue practicing Judaism."[7]

And in Portugal, tens of thousands of others were forcibly converted to Christianity under threat of death. "In 1496, King Manoel of Portugal concluded an agreement to marry Isabel, the daughter of [the 'Catholic Monarchs,' Fernando and Isabel of Spain.] As a condition of the marriage, the Spanish royal family insisted that Portugal expel its Jews as well. King Manoel agreed, although he was reluctant to lose his affluent and accomplished Jewish community."[8]

"Sepharad" is the Hebrew word for Spain, but Sephardic refers to the descendants of Spanish and Portuguese Jews who ended up all over the world:

> For the most part these exiles settled in the countries along the Mediterranean Sea, in the sprawling Turkish Empire, in the Balkans, and in the lands of North Africa. [...] Large groups later settled in the Netherlands, the West Indies, and North America. [...] It was the Sephardim who established the Jewish communities of Curacao in the Caribbean Islands in 1651 and in the Dutch colony of Hamburg, Amsterdam, London, and New Amsterdam (New York City) three years later.[9]

Many Jews who were forced to convert kept Jewish practices in secret. Even those who were exiled were not immune to persecution; many converted to Catholicism while continuing their Jewish practices underground or weaving their Jewish practices into their Catholicism. Anusim (Hebrew, meaning "the coerced") refers to the descendants of forced converts. Five hundred years after the Inquisition, Anusim are still examining their non-traditional Catholic practices and realizing the origins are Jewish. Growing numbers of Anusim are returning to their ancestors' Judaism. There is some controversy about how Anusim should return to Jewish life. Some undergo return ceremonies, although others, like Rabbi Viñas, himself of Cuban descent, recommends that returnees convert under Orthodox supervision, as any additional scrutiny or rejection may be painful for those Anusim who experience internalized fear from the past.

Although the majority of Jews in Latin America are Sephardic, more recently, in 1966, Segundo Villanueva, a Catholic leader of a group of Peruvian Incas, began studying the Torah as a Christian and decided that Jewish traditions were closer to God's commandments. He began teaching Jewish customs to others in his community, and they eventually abandoned Catholicism and adopted Orthodox Jewish practices. Calling themselves the B'nei Moshe ("Children of Moses"), 300 members underwent formal conversion, and made *aliyah* to Israel in the 1990s, with only a small community remaining in Peru.

As of 2005, some 100 members of the B'nei Moshe remain in Cajamarca, Trujillo, and Lima. The Jerusalem-based organization Shavei Israel sent a teacher in 2005 to help the rest of the community prepare for conversion with the goal of enabling them to make aliyah to Israel.[10]

Mizrahi Jews

The term "Mizrahi," which means "Eastern," dates from the time of the establishment of the State of Israel and refers to Jews from a wide range of unrelated Arab Jewish communities. Mizrahi Jews are of Middle East origin and generally self-identify as "Arab Jews," or by their country of origin, e.g. "Iraqi Jew," "Tunisian Jew," "Iranian Jew," etc., and retain particular traditions and practices. Many Mizrahi now follow the liturgical traditions of the

Sephardi and are sometimes colloquially referred to as Sephardic Jews. Many Mizrahi may consider it culturally inaccurate to label them as Sephardic, even if some Mizrahi themselves have come to accept this generalized classification.[11]

Until their forced exile after the birth of the State of Israel, there had been an uninterrupted presence of large Jewish communities in Arab lands from time immemorial, and the history of Jews with origins in North African and Middle Eastern countries like Morocco, Tunisia, Yemen, Iran, and Iraq was one of maintaining Jewish identities despite centuries of intermittent prosperity and persecution:

> The eighth and sixth centuries B.C.E.,[12] when Assyria and Babylon respectively conquered the ancient Kingdoms of Israel and Judea, marked the beginnings of the ancient Jewish communities of the Middle East and North Africa, some 1,000 years before the Arab Muslim conquests of the these regions—including the Land of Israel—and about 2,500 years before the birth of the modern Arab states. [...]

> The 1,400-year history of the Jews under Arab and Muslim rule is a long and varied one. Jews (and Christians) were considered *dhimmi*, a "protected" group of second-class citizens. The Jews' sojourn in Muslim lands was marked by some golden periods of prosperity, when Jews served as advisors to the ruling class; these periods were often marked by Jewish advances in medicine, business, and culture. Jewish philosophy and religious study also flourished. Often, however, the Jews were subjected to punishing taxes, forced to live in cramped ghetto-like quarters and relegated to the lower-levels of the economic and social strata.[13]

There once was a vibrant presence of nearly one million Jews residing in ten Arab countries. Today, however, 99% of this ancient population no longer resides in the lands where they lived for thousands of years. "Jews were stripped of their citizenship in

Egypt, Iraq, Algeria, and Libya; detained or arrested in Algeria, Yemen, Syria, Libya, Iraq, and Egypt; deprived of employment by government decrees in Egypt, Iraq, Libya, Syria, Yemen, and Algeria, and had their property confiscated in all of the Arab lands except Morocco, according to Justice for Jews from Arab Countries (JJAC),[14] one of a number of organizations actively raising the awareness of the plight of Arab Jews.[15]

Such was the fate of the Jews of Iraq, for example. "In 1941, a pro-Nazi government orchestrated anti-Jewish riots that left 200 dead and thousands injured. [M]ore than 135,000 Jews fled an increasingly intolerant Iraq in 1950 and 1951, with little more than the clothes on their backs. [Named Operation Ezra and Nehemiah,] it was a mass exodus—the largest human airlift operation in history."[16] As a result, an estimated 300,000 Iraqi Jews and their descendants now live in Israel and 40,000 live elsewhere.

Recently, JJAC congratulated the Iraqi people and Iraq's Governing Council on the adoption of the "Law of Administration for the State of Iraq for the Transitional Period" signed in Baghdad on March 8, 2004, which states that "any Iraqi whose Iraqi citizenship was withdrawn for political, religious, racial, or sectarian reasons has the right to reclaim his Iraqi citizenship." Some see these developments as harbingers of welcome change. "'It appears that the stage has been set for a new system of justice and the rule of law,' stated S. Daniel Abraham, founding chairman of Justice for Jews from Arab Countries. 'We hope that this signals the beginning of a process to rectify historical injustices and discriminatory measures perpetrated by previous Iraq regimes.'"[17]

According to Jimena's Semha Alwaya, a Jew of Iraqi origin, "Since 1949, the United Nations has passed more than 100 resolutions on Palestinian refugees. Yet, for Jewish refugees from Arab countries not a single U.N. resolution has been introduced recognizing our mistreatment or calling for justice for the hundreds of thousands of Jewish refugees forced out of our homes.[...] It's time for Arab countries to acknowledge that Jews in the Middle East were kicked out of their homelands."[18]

Another advocacy group, the International Federation of Jewish Refugees from Muslim-Arab Countries, based in France and created by Yves-Victor Kamami, is collecting eyewitness accounts of Arab Jews. Rather than the term "refugees," Kamami prefers "an exchange of populations"—referring to the seven hundred thousand Palestinians who left or were forced out in 1948, less than the number Jews who were forced out of Arab lands.[19] As a result, few Jews (or Christians for that matter) remain in Arab lands.

This includes Yemen, a small but dynamic Jewish community that thrived in Yemen for millennia, clinging to Jewish tradition even under adverse conditions. Professor Isaac explains that Yemenite Jews, or "Temani" in Hebrew, are great religious scholars, the only Jewish people in the world who read the Hebrew Bible aloud accompanied by the recitation of the Aramaic Targum, according to the ancient synagogue custom described in the Talmud.[20]

Although Yemenite Jews faced discrimination, they ranked relatively high within the tribal system of Yemen and those who spoke Arabic adapted well to their environment, flourishing economically as professional goldsmiths, silversmiths and managers of the Royal Mint. In spite of the pressure of Yemeni religious leaders' to expel the Jews, the government refrained from drastic actions due to economic considerations. In 1949-50, Operation Magic Carpet, a secret operation that was not made public until several months after it was over, brought 50,000 Yemenite Jews to the newly established State of Israel, where they are now estimated to number around 200,000. There are an estimated 500 to 1,000 Jews left in Yemen, where they live in relative harmony with their Muslim neighbors.[21]

Jews of Africa

When Ethiopian-born Ephraim Isaac is greeted with the question familiar to many diverse Jews, "Are you Jewish? You don't look Jewish," he sometimes responds, "Ethiopia is mentioned in the Bible over 50 times, but Poland not once."[22] Yet, relative to the scholarship about European Jews, little is known about the African Jewish Diaspora. More rigorous scholarship about Jewish migration in Africa is needed, and such studies are being designed and implemented by the Center for Afro-Jewish Studies at Temple University in partnership with the Institute for Jewish & Community Research.

Existing research shows that over the centuries, while Jews migrated north, east, and west, they also went south throughout Africa:

> Pressed under sweeping regional conflicts, Jews settled as traders and warriors in Yemen, the Horn of Africa, Egypt, the Kingdom of Kush and Nubia, North African Punic settlements (Carthage and Velubilis), and areas now covered by Mauritania. More emigrants followed these early Jewish settlers to Northern Africa following the Assyrian conquest of the Israelites in the 8th century B.C.E., and again 200 years later, when Jerusalem was conquered by the Babylonians, leading to the destruction of the First Temple.
>
> The Jewish presence in Africa began to expand significantly in the second and third centuries of the Christian era, extending not only into the Sahara desert, but also reaching down along the West African coast, and possibly also to some Bantu tribes of Southern Africa. [...]
>
> In addition, Jewish, Arab, and Christian accounts cite the existence of Jewish rulers of certain tribal groups and clans identifying themselves as Jewish scattered throughout Mauritania, Senegal, the Western Sudan, Nigeria, and Ghana.[23]

The African story parallels that of other groups of Jews throughout the Diaspora. In Africa, as in other places around the world, there are long-standing communities with greater or lesser degrees of continuous practice, depending on how safe they were. There are those who have Jewish heritage and now practice other religions. Either through assimilation or through forced conversion, some may live as Christians or Muslims and have little sense of their Jewish past. However, others live as Christians or Muslims, yet are proud of their Jewish ancestry. There are also those who discovered Judaism and decided to convert to Judaism. These are more recent newcomers to the Jewish people.

Whether ancient or new, a distinctive trait of African communities results from historical isolation from rabbinic Judaism. Their Judaism has either been passed on through oral tradition or is practiced as pre-Talmudic Torah-based Judaism.[24] These communities would like to be part of world Judaism.

The Lost Tribes of Israel

Some Africans have ancient Jewish heritage and consider themselves descendants of the "Lost Tribes" of Israel. Around 926 B.C.E., the kingdom of Israel split in two. Previously, all twelve tribes of Israel had been united under the monarchies of Saul, David, and Solomon. But when Solomon's son Rehoboam ascended to the throne, the ten northern tribes rebelled and seceded from the union. This left only two tribes—Judah and Benjamin—under the control of the king in Jerusalem. From that time on, the tribes were divided into two nations, which came to be called the House of Israel (the ten northern tribes) and the House of Judah (the two southern tribes).

When the Assyrians conquered the House of Israel around 722 B.C.E., they deported the native populations to other places throughout the Assyrian kingdom. Many Israelites made their way across the Silk Road ending up in Asia and Africa, where they intermarried with the peoples among whom they settled. They eventually abandoned their distinct identity, and their culture was lost to history. These are the groups are referred to as the "Lost Tribes" of Israel.

> There are quite a number of peoples today who cling to the ancient tradition that they are descended from the Jewish Lost Tribes: the tribesmen of Afghanistan, the Mohammedan Berbers of West Africa, and the six million Christian Igbo people of Nigeria. Unquestionably, they all practice certain ancient Hebraic customs and beliefs, which lends some credibility to their fantastic-sounding claims."[25]

An Israeli organization, Amishav ("My People Returns"), founded in Israel in 1975 with the encouragement of Rabbi Zvi Yehuda Kook, is directed by Rabbi Eliyahu Avichail, who has devoted his life to traveling around the world searching for people who, though not formally Jewish, observe many Jewish customs. Michael Freund founded Shavei Israel in 2004 to expand the work inspired by Rabbi Avichail. If they encounter groups with compelling evidence and the desire to re-embrace Judaism, then these organizations help individuals undergo Orthodox conversion and settle in Israel. According to conversion advocate Lawrence Epstein, Rabbi Avichail distinguishes between the conversions that occur for these presumed members of the Lost Tribes and the conversions of gentiles:

> Normally, potential converts are turned away and told to return after a period of time so that the prospective Jew can offer convincing evidence of sincerity. For Marranos [perjorative term for Anusim] and remnants of the Lost Tribes, who presumably have remnants of a Jewish soul, however, Rabbi Avichail believes no such discouragement is called for. In fact, for the rabbi, the formal act of conversion is simply "to bring back people with a Jewish past," and is not a typical conversion. [26]

African Jewish Communities

Jewish communities have existed throughout Africa for centuries. Some are ancient, some more recent, and others once existed but are now extinct. The following section briefly describes some of those communities to illustrate both the historical roots and the possibilities for the future of the Jewish people.

Ancient
North Africa (Egypt, Morocco, Tunisia, & Algeria)
Beta Israel, Ethiopia
Lemba, southern Africa

Newer (some with ancient heritage)
Abayudaya, Uganda
Igbo/Ibo, Nigeria
House of Israel, Ghana
Kenya

Extinct
Timbuktu, Mali
Cape Verde
São Tome & Principe

North Africa: Egypt, Morocco, Tunisia, & Algeria

North African, or "Maghrebi" Jews of Egypt, Morocco, Tunisia, and Algeria, maintained their faith for more than two thousand years, in some instances surviving violence, political and geographic segregation, and legal status as second-class citizens. After the birth of the State of Israel in 1948, most North African Jews were expelled from their places of birth, along with other Mizrahi Jews from Arab states in the Middle East. Some countries still have an active, albeit small contingent of Jews who still practice a unique form of distinctly North African Judaism.

During British rule and under King Fuad, Egypt was somewhat more friendly towards its Jewish population. Although they were not allowed to claim Egyptian nationality, Jews played important roles in the economy. Of the 100,000 Jews who lived in Egypt before 1948, only a hundred or so remain today. Many Egyptian Jews fled to Israel (35,000), with the rest going to Brazil, France, the United States and Argentina. Today, anti-Semitism is common in the Egyptian media.[27]

The Jewish community of Morocco had a peak population of 300,000 Jews before 1948. In the midst of the first Arab-Israeli war, riots against Jews broke out, and they began leaving for Israel. In 1955, when Morocco attained independence, Jews occupied several political positions, including three seats in parliament and a ministry. The Six-Day War in 1967 led to increased Arab-Jewish tensions worldwide, and by 1971 the Jewish population was down to 35,000. As of 2004, Marrakesh had an aging population of about 260 people, most over the age of 60, while around 3,000 Jews remained in Casablanca.

Despite their small numbers, Jews continue to play a notable role in Morocco: the king retains a Jewish senior adviser, and Jewish schools and synagogues receive government subsidies. However, Jewish targets have sometimes been attacked (notably in Al-Qaeda's bombing of a Jewish community center in Casablanca in 2003), and there is sporadic anti-Semitic rhetoric from radical Moslem groups. However, King Mohammed VI is taking an assertive stand against Islamic radicalism and reaffirmed the protection his predecessors historically offered to Morocco's Jews.[28]

Tunisia has had a Jewish minority since Roman times. The Jewish community of Tunisia received successive waves of immigration over time, mostly from Spain and Portugal at the times of the Inquisition and then from Italy. In 1948 the Jewish population was an estimated 105,000, but by 1967 most Tunisian Jews had left the country for France and Israel, and the population had shrunk to 20,000. As of 2004, an estimated 1,500 remained, particularly on the island of Djerba, noted for its ancient synagogues, and in Tunis where most Jews still live as they have for centuries, maintaining strict Jewish practices and surviving by metalworking and jewelry-making. In the last few decades, a small but deadly number of attacks against Jews have occurred; however, they are generally not regarded as state sponsored and the Islamic government allows freedom of worship to the Jewish community.[29]

Jews have a long history in Algeria. In the 14th century, with the deterioration of conditions in Spain, many Spanish Jews moved to Algeria. After the French occupation of the country in 1830, Jews gradually adopted French culture and were granted French citizenship in 1870. Most of Algeria's 140,000 Jews left the country for France when Algeria attained independence in 1962. Following the brutal conflict of the Armed Islamic Group's 1994 declaration of war on all non-Muslims in the country, most of the thousand-odd remaining Jews left. A single synagogue functions in Algiers, although there is no rabbi. All other synagogues have been taken over for use as mosques.[30]

Beta Israel, Ethiopia

The group of African Jews that has received the most attention in mainstream media is the *Beta Israel*, the Jews of Ethiopia, a 2,500-year-old biblically Jewish community. The Beta Israel have become so well known that some Jews may think that *any* dark-skinned Jew is Ethiopian. Although the central legend of Beta Israel Judaism is the story of King Solomon and Queen Sheba, historians trace Ethiopian Jewish ancestry to the tribe of Dan, which migrated through the Nile valley to the ancient African kingdom of Cush.

The Beta Israel are often referred to as *Falasha*, meaning "stranger" in Ge'ez, the classical ecclesiastical tongue of Ethiopia, a derogatory term descriptive of their community's status as outsiders since the 4th century, when King Ezana declared Christianity the official religion of his kingdom.

Because of rescue missions Operation Moses (1984-85), Operation Joshua (1985), and Operation Solomon (1991), 100,000 Beta Israel now have Jewish lives in Israel. What most Jews do not know is that the process to recognize Ethiopian Jews as "real" and "legitimate" took well over 100 years, and the struggle is not over. Thousands of "Falash Mura," Ethiopian Jews who, like Anusim, were forced to convert to Christianity and want to return to Judaism, remain in camps in Addis Ababa and in remote northern villages of Gondar, waiting to be accepted as legitimate Jews and make aliyah to Israel. Although movement toward recognition finally seems achievable, this path also has been tortuously slow.[31]

Lemba, Southern Africa

There have long been many sub-Saharan African communities. Some are dispersed and have found it difficult to maintain their connections to their religious pasts. The geographic challenges are often coupled with aggressive missionary pressures from messianic Jews,[32] Christians, and Muslims. For example, the Lemba of South Africa, Zimbabwe, and Mozambique have always been aware and are fiercely proud of their Jewish ancestry, but they do not necessarily practice Judaism today. This may be changing, as some leaders of the community, including Rabson Wuriga, Ph.D., and members of the Lemba Cultural Association (LCA), are attempting to organize and educate dispersed individuals and reclaim the practice of Judaism among a wider segment of the Lemba population.

There are Lemba who live in urban centers, well-educated professionals and academics. At the same time, they may be the tribal elders who maintain a closely guarded oral Lemba history. Though non-Lemba women are allowed to marry into the tribe, Lemba men face expulsion if they marry gentiles. According to Dr. Rudo Mathivha, daughter of Professor M.E.R. Mathivha, the late president of the LCA, the Lemba are descended from a group of Jews who left Judea in approximately 500 B.C.E. and settled first in Yemen before traveling south through Africa.[33] The story of their long migration through Ethiopia, Tanzania, Kenya, Malawi, Mozambique, Zimbabwe, and South Africa has been retained and passed down through oral tradition.

A *60 Minutes* segment, featuring Tudor Parfitt, head of the Judaic Studies department at the University of London, reported the results of DNA testing showing both Semitic origins of the Lemba in general and the now well-known existence of a marker associated with the Kohanim on the Y chromosome of many Lemba males, although DNA cannot necessarily prove or disprove Jewish origins.[34] The testing itself remains controversial among the Lemba, with some feeling vindicated by the results as scientific proof of their Jewish roots, while others are insulted by the very idea of having to prove their identity. In response to those who question his legitimacy as a Jew, Wuriga responds, "My father told me I am a Jew. To whom am I going to listen? I am going to listen to my father."[35]

Abayudaya, Uganda

Other communities have found their way to Judaism only in the last hundred years. In Uganda, the Abayudaya, whose tribal name means "people of Judah," trace their Jewish origins to the turn of the 20th century. According to Rabbi Gershom Sizomu, their spiritual leader, the Abayudaya began their journey to Judaism under the leadership of Semei Kakungulu. He was a great warrior who cooperated with the British, but who ultimately became disillusioned when his political aspirations were ignored. The disagreements that Kakungulu had with the British administration ultimately caused him to break away from Christianity and brought him closer to the Hebrew Bible. In 1919, he took on the task of circumcising himself along with his sons and urged others to do the same. They began practicing the Torah-based Judaism that they maintain to this day. Over the years, Kakungulu's knowledge of Judaism increased as a result of meeting several Jews, who instructed the Abayudaya in Jewish practice and Hebrew, and left them with a Hebrew/English bible. Kakungulu died in Mbale on November 24, 1928, by which time the Abayudaya numbered approximately 2,000.[36]

Since then, as has happened to so many other groups of Jews, the community has at times been subject to governmental pressures to abandon their Jewish practices. In 1971, Idi Amin came to power, banning Jewish practice and ordering Jews to convert to Christianity or Islam. Some did convert, and others were murdered; still, approximately 600 members of the Abayudaya community have persisted for three generations, living in six villages in the green, rolling hills of eastern Uganda, near Mbale, where, like other rural Ugandans, they support themselves primarily through subsistence farming.[37]

Rabbi Sizomu and his brother JJ Keki were leaders of the "Kibbutz Movement" in the early 1980s, reclaiming the land and building a synagogue (the "Moses" synagogue), which restored the Abayudaya community's focus. The Abayudaya keep a respectful distance from non-Jews in matters of religion, but they mingle with their Christian and Muslim neighbors at home, in the market, and in all other areas of public life. Mr. Keki, a successful farmer, became the first elected Jewish public official in the region of 80,000.

Even though the Abayudaya regard themselves as Jews, they realized that their isolation from the Jewish world had prevented them from gaining a more thorough understanding of Judaism. At their request, with the help of Kulanu, an organization dedicated to lost Jewish communities, a beit din from the Conservative movement went to Uganda in 2002 to formally convert most of the Abayudaya community. Over the last ten years, the Abayudaya have developed significant relationships with Jews around the world, and life is changing for the community. Some Abayudaya youth have begun attending university and hope to become engineers, doctors, teachers, and rabbis.

It was the dream of Rabbi Sizomu to attend rabbinic school in the United States. The Institute for Jewish & Community Research sponsored the Sizomu family to live in Los Angeles and Israel for five years while he attended the Ziegler School of Rabbinic Studies at the University of Judaism. As of this printing, Rabbi Sizomu's goal, upon his return to Uganda, is to open a yeshiva to serve African Jews.

Ibo/Igbo, Nigeria

Some recent returnees to the Jewish people have ancient roots. The Ibo (or Igbo) are a tribe in Nigeria numbering in the millions. Remy Illona writes in his 2005 book about the history of the Ibo:

> The Ibo Benei-Yisrael of Nigeria [...] are an ethnic group [that] descended from the southern and westward migrations of both ancient Hebrew and later Israeli peoples from the Middle East into Africa. [...] The oral traditions of the Ibo maintain that their presence has been in what is termed "Iboland" for over 1,500 years. [They] state that their ancestors were migrants from ancient Israel, possibly beginning with the Semitic migrations from Northern Arabia into Eastern Africa around 500 B.C.E..[38]

Ibo oral tradition references the names of specific Lost Tribes from which these clans are believed to have originated. However, many Ibo have no awareness of their Jewish heritage. Others are aware and proud of their Jewish ancestry and are actively reclaiming Judaism. Certain Nigerian Jewish communities have been making increasing connections with world Jewry. There are relatively recent efforts to reestablish the Jewish community in Nigeria, including building synagogues. Rabbi Capers Funnye's congregation in Chicago, represented by Nigerian-born Dele Jane

Osawe, is sponsoring the building of a sister synagogue in Delta State, Nigeria. Because no formal census has been taken in the region, it is unknown how many native Jews reside in Nigeria. There may be twenty-six synagogues of various sizes and estimates of possibly as many as 30,000 Ibos practicing some form of Judaism. Further research is necessary.

House of Israel, Ghana

The House of Israel, centered in the southwestern towns of Sefwi Wiawso and Sefwi Sui, is a relatively new Jewish community, but one that may have ancient roots. In 1976, a Ghanaian man named Aaron Ahomtre Toakyirafa recognized that the traditions of his Sefwi ancestors were similar to traditions of ancient Jews. Their story is typical of many communities in Africa: Before Christian missionaries converted much of Ghana nearly a hundred years ago, the Sefwi people practiced many "unusual" traditions, such as adherence to Saturday as a day of rest, dietary restrictions that forbade them from eating pork, the circumcision in youth of male community members, and the isolation of women in the community during their menstrual cycle.

Toakyirafa, along with his neighbor, David Ahenkorah, and others, researched their community and traced their historical origins from ancient Israel, through Mali, the Ivory Coast, wandering throughout West Africa to escape persecution, to their present home in Ghana. Convinced of their Jewish origins, Toakyirafa began to teach about Judaism. After he died in 1991, many thought that Judaism would disappear from the community, but in 1993 Ahenkorah became community leader. He re-affirmed the community's Jewish identity, reinstituted open Jewish practice, and built a synagogue.[39]

Kenya

An agrarian African Jewish community in Kenya is in transition to Judaism. Mr. Keki, from the Abayudaya community in neighboring Uganda, has traveled to Kenya several times with the goal of helping to support this emerging Jewish community. They are eager for contact with other Jews and as a result have sent a few of their students to study in the school of the more developed Abayudaya Jewish community in Uganda.

Timbuktu, Mali

There are several thousand people of unquestioned Jewish ancestry in Timbuktu, Mali. Egyptian Jews began trading with tribes in the northern part of Mali as long ago as biblical times and pushed further and further into the Sahara throughout the centuries. In the eighth century, the Rhadanites (multi-lingual Jewish traders) settled in Timbuktu and used it as a base from which they could solidify their trade routes through the desert. In the 14th and 15th centuries, Jews fleeing Spanish persecution settled in Timbuktu. In 1492, King Askia Muhammed took power in Timbuktu and threatened Jews with execution who did not convert to Islam. Some Jews fled, some converted, and some remained in Mali, suffering centuries of persecution. By the 20th century there were no practicing Jews in Mali.

However, Malian Jewry has begun to experience a revival. In 1993, Ismael Diadie Haidara, a historian from Timbuktu, established Zakhor (the Timbuktu Association for Friendship with the Jewish World) for the almost one thousand Malian descendants of Jews who have become interested in exploring their identity. Zakhor's members hope to teach their children about their Jewish heritage and revive their interest in Judaism.[40]

Cape Verde

In 1496 when the Portuguese expelled the Jews from their land and forced others to convert, many *Cristãos Novos* ("New Christians") escaped to places like the islands of Cape Verde, the refueling stop on the Atlantic Ocean route to the New World.

There they worked as merchants and in some cases slave traders, hiding their Judaism for generations. Ultimately, they stopped practicing Judaism in any form. Descendants of the Portuguese Cristãos Novos and the Moroccan-Jewish Cape Verdeans founded the Cape Verde-Israel Friendship Society in 1995 in order to revitalize Jewish life on the islands.[41]

São Tome and Principe

In the late 1400s, King Manoel I of Portugal imposed a head tax on Jews to finance his colonial aspirations. When some Jews refused to pay the tax, the king punished them by deporting almost 2,000 Jewish children, ages 2-10, to two small islands off the west coast of Africa, São Tome and Principe; only 600 were alive a year later. Some of the surviving Jewish children retained some semblance of their parents' religion. Observances generally declined, but in the 19th and 20th centuries some Jewish traders arrived on the islands and seeded a small new community. Today there are no known practicing Jews on the islands, but the descendants of these exiled children have expressed interest in learning more about the customs of their ancestors.[42]

Jews of India

Jews in India have lived among the predominant Hindu and Muslim population for millennia, making Judaism one of the oldest religions in India. Over the centuries, the Jews preserved their customs and traditions while assimilating with the local population. Unlike many parts of the world, Jews have lived in India without significant violence or anti-Semitism, and have been accorded an honorable place in the social structure. In Mumbai (formerly Bombay), two synagogues are located in predominantly Muslim areas, with no record of ill-will between the two communities. Even so, economic factors, among others, have prompted many Jews to emigrate to Britain, Australia, Canada, the United

States, and Israel. Never a large community, the Jewish population remaining in India was estimated to number around 5,000 in the year 2000. There are four major groupings of Jews in India, each with its own unique history. They are the Cochin Jews, the Baghdadi Jews, the Bene Israel, and the B'nei Menashe.[43]

Cochin Jews (Malabar Jews)

The oldest of the Jewish communities, the Cochin Jews arrived in India 2,500 years ago. Several rounds of immigration from the Jewish Diaspora to the southern state of Kerala led to a diversity amongst the Cochin Jews. The biggest group is called "Meyuhassim" ("privileged" in Hebrew) or Malabar Jews. The forebears of these Jews are considered to have arrived in India during the period of King Solomon. The second group is called "Pardesi" ("foreigner" in some Indian languages), who came to Kerala at different periods from different countries: Egypt, Iraq, Syria, Iran, Spain, and Germany. These two groups were successful merchants and had slaves who were converted to Judaism. They were released from their status as slaves and are called "Meshuhararim" ("released" in Hebrew).

In 1524, they moved from the port of Cranganore (now called Kudungallur) further south to Cochin to escape attacks from the Moors and the Portuguese. The Jews fled to Cochin under the protection of a Hindu Raja who granted them their own area of the city, later called "Jew Town." The Cochini Jews at their height in the 1940s numbered 3,000. Although most Cochin Jews have emigrated primarily to Israel or elsewhere, a small population of mainly elderly men and women still inhabit "Jew Town."[44]

Baghdadi Jews

The most recent arrivals are the Baghdadi Jews (sometimes called "Iraqi Jews") who came to India as traders and religiously persecuted refugees 250 years ago from West Asia—Iraq, Iran,

Afghanistan, Syria, and Yemen. Most of the "Baghdadis" were successful merchants and businessmen and quickly became successful leaders in Mumbai and Calcutta. As philanthropists, they built hospitals, schools, libraries, and monuments in many cities of India. For the most part, however, the Baghdadi Jews remained separate from Indian society, including other Indian Jews, preferring to identify with British culture.

The Baghdadis at their height numbered about 7,000 in the 1940s, although today there are less than 200 left in India, most of them having emigrated to Britain, Australia, and Canada.

Bene Israel

At the present, the Bene Israel predominate the Jewish presence in India. Their story is an old one, but like many ancient communities, it is the subject of scholarly dispute. According to oral tradition, the Bene Israel are descended from Jews who escaped persecution from the Syrian-Greek ruler Antiochus Epiphan in 175 B.C.E. A shipwreck stranded seven Jewish families at Navgaon near the port of Cheul on the Konkan Coast, thirty miles south of Mumbai. The families multiplied and integrated with the local Maharashtrian population, adopting their language, dress, and food, and became physically indistinguishable from the local population.

However, the Bene Israel were clearly differentiated from others because of their adherence to Judaism. The Bene Israel say their ancestors were oil pressers in the Galilee, hence their nickname *shanwar teli* ("Saturday oil-pressers"), given by the local population because they abstained from work on Shabbat. They remained isolated from mainstream Judaism until the 19th century when Cochin and Baghdadi Jews became involved in training the Bene Israel religious leadership. The Bene Israel were encouraged to move to Mumbai for better employment opportunities. Over time, the Bene Israel community became successful, producing distinguished military leaders, doctors, lawyers, and other professionals.

It is estimated that there were 6,000 Bene Israel in the 1830s, 10,000 at the turn of the century, and in 1948 they numbered 20,000. When the British withdrew from India in 1947, and the State of Israel was established in 1948, the Bene Israel began to emigrate to Israel. About 60,000 Bene Israel live in Israel today. In 1964, the Israeli Rabbinate declared that the Bene Israel are "full Jews in every respect." There are approximately 2,000 living in United States and elsewhere.[46]

According to Romiel Daniel, a Mumbai-born Jew who serves as president and occasional cantor for the Rego Park Jewish Center in Queens, New York:

> There are 29 synagogues in Mumbai, in a country with about 5,000 Jews. [...] Most Indian Jews were traders and merchants, and throughout their long history in the country they enjoyed tranquil relations with their Hindu neighbors.[47]

The Bene Israel adhere to their own traditions and rites. Like the Lemba of South Africa, a DNA test in 2002 confirmed that the Bene Israel share the same heredity as the Kohanim.[48]

B'nei Menashe

In northeast India, in the land mass that lies between Myanmar (formerly Burma) and Bangladesh, a small group of people have been practicing Judaism since the early 1970s, having returned to the religion of their ancestors. The B'nei Menashe are Mizo and Kuki tribesmen in Manipur and Mizoram who believe that they are descended from the ancient tribe of Menashe. Evidence shows that after the exile of 722 B.C.E., many Israelites made their way across the Silk Road, ending up in China. The Shinlung tribe, as they were called in China, eventually migrated to Burma and northeast India, losing many of their Jewish customs along the way. Although their "leather scrolls" were destroyed, the B'nei Menashe still held on to their oral history and the poems describing their ancestors crossing the Red Sea. After thousands of years of exile, they have rediscovered their roots and are returning to Judaism.

While over 300 have formally converted to Judaism and many of these have moved to Israel, thousands of others live fully Jewish lives without having yet converted. In a historic decision, Sephardic Chief Rabbi Shlomo Amar has formally recognized the Bnei Menashe community of northeastern India as "descendants of Israel" and has agreed to send a Beit Din on its behalf to the region to formally convert them to Judaism.[50] In a recent turn of events, Rabbi Ekstein, founder of the International Fellowship of Christians and Jews, has informed the government of Israel that his organization would provide the $8 million to settle the 6,000 Bnei Menashe in Israel, citing the recent certification of authenticity by the Sephardic chief rabbi of Israel.

In a July 2005 *New York Times* magazine article, Zev Chafets, founding editor of *Jerusalem Report*, touches upon the complexity of Israeli politics and the implications of settling the B'nei Menashe in Israel for other communities:

> Transporting 6,000 lost Jews from India to Israel is [...] a political act. Israeli political parties will tussle over patronage of this new voting bloc. Right-wingers will fight to get it housed in the West Bank; left-wingers will try to prevent that. And the Palestinians will condemn the whole exercise as a Zionist trick to upset the demographic balance.[51]

Chafets captures a fear shared ironically by both sides of the spectrum—those who are concerned with preserving the authenticity of the Jewish people as well as those who advocate for the dissolution of the Jewish people: "If a rabbi can turn 6,000 Indians into biblical Jews and take them to Israel, what's to stop him from finding 600,000 somewhere else?" Some communities of Jews, who are either persecuted or who are extremely isolated, may need to take refuge in Israel, such as the Beta Israel from Ethiopia. However, other communities, both historical, like the Lemba, or new, like the Abayudaya, want to remain where they are. They would like to be able to apply for a visa to visit or study in Israel without undue suspicion, or have the same rights as other individuals to make aliyah as they chose. They would like to be recognized as Jews, without becoming embroiled in Jewish communal politics or the brunt of the "explosive" politics of the Middle East. Their goal is to practice Judaism, not necessarily to make aliyah.

Jews of China

As with other ancient communities, it is unclear exactly when the Jews first arrived in China. Scholars say that Jews may have come as early as the First Temple period, from the ten Lost Tribes, or during the Talmudic period. At that time, Roman, Persian, and Middle Eastern merchants came to China for trade. Jewish merchants may have traveled the Silk Road to Kaifeng to conduct trade and stayed there for better business opportunities.

There are traces of a Jewish presence beginning at least in the 7th century. The first documented proof of Jewish existence in China was discovered over a century ago. A letter written in Judeo-Persian on paper (a commodity that was produced only in China) was found attesting to the fact that the Jews probably came from Persia, introducing cotton-cloth to China, known primarily for its silk industry.

The most enduring community was that in Kaifeng. From the 10th-13th century, China was ruled by the emperors of the Song Dynasty from their capital at Kaifeng, which lies north of Beijing on the Yellow River. It had a population of 1.5 million people in the 10ᵗʰ century, probably the largest city in the world at the time:

> [Kaifeng was] a bustling metropolis straddling the legendary Silk Road that linked their sprawling domain to its trading partners in the West. [...] The main street in the Jewish section of Kaifeng is called The Lane of the Sect that Teaches the Scriptures, the remnants of a Jewish community which flourished for nearly a thousand years until the 1840s.[52]

The synagogue in Kaifeng, constructed in the 11ᵗʰ century, was the center of their life and activities. The 5,000 Jews in 17ᵗʰ century Kaifeng were successful in Confucian society. In the mid-17ᵗʰ century a civil war raged in China, and Kaifeng was flooded, resulting in the destruction of the entire city. Only one-third of the population survived, including some 1,000 Jews. Kaifeng never fully recovered. The Jews rebuilt the synagogue in 1663. During this time, the Kaifeng Jews were discovered by Jesuit priests.

This community finally disintegrated in the 1850s. The community began to dwindle due to a lack of rabbis, loss of proficiency in Hebrew, a lack of a Chinese Torah translation, and the repeated destruction of the synagogue by Yellow River floods. The remaining Jews could not maintain the synagogue, and were forced to sell the building and manuscripts to Protestant missionaries. The Jews integrated into Chinese society and assimilated. Yet, there still are descendants who feel a link to Judaism.[53]

Baghdadi Jews established a Sephardi community in Shanghai after the opening of the Treaty Ports in 1845. Shanghai's small Jewish community became a safe haven where Jews were allowed to practice Judaism freely and even build their own autonomous government:

> The ghetto, in what was once the American and then the International Settlement and is now called the North

Bund, harbored more than 20,000 Jews who fled Nazi Europe from 1933 to 1941 and another 5,000 to 10,000 who fled Stalin's Russia before that. Viewers of Steven Spielberg's 1987 film *Empire of the Sun* got a glimpse of the area. Known in Chinese as Hongkou (or Hongkew), the ghetto was a haven for stateless refugees in a city that for years did not require a visa to enter.[54]

Later, Russian Jews escaping pogroms founded Jewish communities in Harbin in the northeast of China. Davi Cheng, a Chinese Jew from Los Angeles, remembers that her mother, who grew up in Harbin, used to tell her about her Russian friends. According to Li Shuxiao, vice director of Jewish research at the Heilongjiang Academy of Social Sciences:

> The first Jew reportedly arrived in Harbin around 1899, leading what would eventually be three waves of immigration. The first group, in the early 20th century, came in search of opportunity after the opening of the Russia-China railroad. The second fled the 1917 Russian Revolution. A third sought to escape a Russia-China border conflict in 1929. The peak was around 1920, when the local Jewish population reached 20,000.[55]

In an effort to stimulate foreign tourism, trade, and business investment in the region, Harbin recently announced a $3.2-million renovation of its main synagogue, other historically significant buildings, and Asia's largest Jewish cemetery.

By the 1950s, most Jews had left China, but the buildings they created, the records they kept, their economic and their cultural contributions are a monument to that historical experience. Since 1986, Professor Xu Xin of Nanjing University, who has been researching, lecturing, and writing on Judaism and Jews in China, and the Sino-Judaic Institute, founded in 1985 to serve as a vehicle for the study and preservation of Jewish history in China, are primarily responsible for current education about the Jews in China. The Sino-Judaic Institute deemed it "imperative that a nation of one fifth of the world's population have access to accurate and unbiased materials about Jews."[56]

Conclusion

Some Jews may view the legitimacy of these ancient and emerging diverse communities with a suspicion that borders on outright rejection of the notion that such peoples could be Jewish, as well as African or Asian or ... fill in the blank with any description that means "not what I know." Ignoring, or perhaps never having known that Jews have always been a diverse worldwide people, some Jews treat their discovery of other Jewish communities as anthropological finds. Others are attempting to shed light on the diversity of peoples and practices around the world.[57] Ken Blady's book, *Jewish Communities in Exotic Places*[58] draws attention to some of the more unfamiliar practices of various Jewish groups. His motivation in writing the book is admirable: "Most Jews in the world," he says, "tend to think there are Ashkenazim,

> No matter how long a group has been identifying as Jewish, some Jews may still ask them to prove their legitimacy.

and that anyone who has a permanent suntan is Sephardic. It's a terrible stereotype, and we need to understand who the Jewish people are."[59] Still, despite his good intentions, he and others unwittingly treat living people with living traditions as exotic objects of study rather than as fellow Jews to be integrated into a broader Jewish history and community. Unfortunately, they are in a paradoxical situation: bringing attention to the diversity of the Jewish people can seem by definition like exoticizing them; still it is better to have more, rather than less knowledge about diverse Jews around the world.

A few people have lost patience with the reluctance of the mainstream community to embrace global Jewry. Karen Primack, editor of Kulanu's quarterly newsletter[60] writes that she has "come to appreciate [...] the irony that allows many Jews to wring their hands in despair over the intermarriage rate and yet ignore the plight of our cousins [...] who have maintained their identity through twenty-seven centuries of hardship. Many are practicing Jews eager to study further in Israel, and some to relocate there. They deserve at least as much attention—and financial support—as those who are *leaving* Judaism."[61]

That Jews all over the world share Jewish ritual practices, obvious as this commonality may seem, is sometimes not enough for some Jews to accept communities unfamiliar to them as truly Jewish. No matter how long a group has been identifying as Jewish and practicing a recognizable form of Judaism, some Jews may still ask them to prove their legitimacy.[62] According to Professor Isaac:

> The fact is that today large segments of the Jewish popula-
> tion cannot even count their ancestral lineage [...] beyond
> two or three generations. Jews and ancient converts to
> Judaism have lived all over the world for over two thou-
> sand years, and they should be the last to defend unreal-
> istic Jewish authenticity or the concept of non-existing
> racial or ethnic purity or uniformity.[63]

Jewish law states that a Jew is a person who is either born to Jewish parents (i.e., one who has Jewish "blood") or who converts to Judaism according to the rules of a particular branch of Judaism. Since some communities in question have been in exis-tence for hundreds (or thousands) of years, they do not have the paperwork that proves their lineage or certification from a beit din that shows they were properly converted. Most Jews of European origin do not have such proof, and more importantly, nobody asks for it.

Who Is a Jew?
Ideology and Bloodlines

Questions of legitimacy become particularly important for
Jews of color. Despite their acceptance of Ethiopian Jews, some
white American Jews—out of fear, ignorance, or prejudice—are
less willing to recognize as Jewish the people of color in their own
midst. Racially and ethnically diverse Jews are regularly
subjected to the test of proving that they are *real* Jews instead of
imposters or infiltrators. Do they have papers? Did they convert?
If so, how did they convert? Can they read Hebrew? While many
of these same issues characterize Jewish views of converts and
those that different groups of Jews have of each other, this testing
is more often administered to ethnically and racially diverse Jews,
if only because they appear so different from the majority
community in the United States.

For the many diverse Jews who may be questioned or viewed
with suspicion (or even just with curiosity) by mainstream Jews,
their claim to "authenticity" is based on a deeply resonant idea
fundamental to Judaism: they are Jews because at least one of
their biological parents was Jewish. Simple enough. But, as with
nearly every issue that engages *halakha*, or Jewish law, the question of who qualifies as a "Jewish parent" is deeply complicated

and controversial. In its simplest form, the question may be decided based on the practices of different streams of Judaism. The Orthodox and Conservative movements hold that those children born of Jewish mothers are Jewish (matrilineal descent), regardless of their level of observance. In other words, a Jewish mother's blood means Jewish personhood.

The Reform movement, beginning in 1983, adopted a different policy. They returned to the ancient practice of patrilineal descent, in which "the father had to be an Israelite, contrary to the later halakhic ruling—now the subject of so much controversy—that defines a Jew as the child of a Jewish mother."[1] According to the official website of the Reform movement:

> The Reform position on this question, referred to as Patrilineal Descent, is often misunderstood. What we say is that a child born of one Jewish parent, whether it is the mother or the father, is under the PRESUMPTION of being Jewish, but that his/her Jewishness must be activated by "appropriate and timely" Jewish acts. It is not enough to simply be born to a Jewish parent. For a boy, one such act would certainly be *brit milah*. Without that, one might question this child's Jewishness. If, on the other hand, the family celebrated Jewish holidays, educated the boy, had him become a bar mitzvah, etc., in other words, if the child is being raised exclusively as a Jew and was not baptized and is not being given a formal or informal Christian education, then we would consider him Jewish, just as an Orthodox Jew would consider a boy born of a Jewish mother to be Jewish even if he had not been circumcised.

> Another way to put it is like this: we consider a person who acts and identifies as a Jew to be a Jew, a definition we find happier than a sort of bloodline/racial definition (especially after the Holocaust).

> By the way, when the Reform movement debated this years ago, scholarly papers pointed out that in the Bible

the line ALWAYS followed the father, including the cases
of all those heroes, like Joseph and Moses, who married
into non-Israelite priestly families.[2]

The policy of counting both mothers and fathers as the Jewish
parent grew out of a recognition that the number of children born
of "mixed marriages" in America was growing, while the total
number of Jews was not. This shift by the Reform movement,
along with their official position of supporting outreach towards
non-Jews, represents the movement's attempt to forge an egalitarian and inclusive response to disheartening demographics.
While blood is not the sole determinant of Jewishness for the
Reform movement, it still provides the starting place for confer-

ring institutional legitimacy on
people born of one Jewish and one
non-Jewish parent. Even with the
inclusion of *attitudes* and *behaviors*
in the definition of who is considered a Jew, one cannot get away
from the mythical power of DNA.

> One cannot fall into the
> trap of believing there are
> Jewish genetic traits,
> positive or negative.

Of course, no scientific evidence shows that such a thing as a
"Jewish race" exists. Yes, there are certain genetic markers on the
male Y chromosome thought to be associated with Kohanim (the
same markers found in many male Lemba in South Africa). Some
genetic commonality, however, does not equal race.

Many Jews are ambivalent, even contradictory, when it
comes to bloodline. On the one hand, positive traits like intelli-
gence are considered by some Jews to be "in the genes." Some go
as far as to say that one cannot be Jewish without a specific
genetic history. On the other hand, most Jews vehemently
oppose the notion that they are a racial group. One should not
fall into the trap of believing there are Jewish genetic traits,
positive or negative.

It is a dangerous and troubling line of reasoning to believe that Jews are biologically different from others, that there are Jewish genes and Jewish blood. Do Jewish genes result in recognizably Jewish physical attributes? Is there Jewish hair, a Jewish skin tone, a Jewish laugh? Funny or not, either none of us looks Jewish, or all of us do.

Whether Jewish blood is the single determinant or part of a more complex definition of who is a Jew, this emphasis on Jewish lineage has immense and far-reaching implications, crossing from issues of individual identity and legitimacy to larger questions of social and political structures and of worldwide migration of peoples. If such a thing as Jewish blood exists, then what does that imply about the people of color (or white Jews for that matter) who have been practicing Judaism for generations without any of their forebears having undergone a formal conversion? What about the millions of people whose ancestors were forced to convert to Christianity or Islam, and want to return to Judaism? How many years must a people identify as Jews, follow Jewish law, and claim a connection with Jewish history before mainstream Jewish institutions and individuals consider them to have Jewish blood? What about people or groups who do undergo formal conversion, yet who are not always accepted either, even after twenty years or two hundred years? What is the statute of limitations blocking legitimacy?

In the United States, vibrant and long-established communities of African Americans have been practicing Judaism parallel to the mainstream Jewish community for many decades. According to Rabbi Capers Funnye:

> The International Israelite Board of Rabbis represents the oldest and largest denomination of black Jews. Rabbi Wentworth Arthur Matthew (1862-1973) and Rabbi Arnold Joshua Ford (1877-1935) founded our first congregations in Harlem. Rabbi Matthew's congregation,

Commandment Keepers, was established in 1919, and
Rabbi Ford's congregation, called Beth B'nai Abraham,
was established in 1924. In 1930, Rabbi Matthew established the Israelite Rabbinical Academy. The goal of the
school was to train and ordain men to serve the black
Jewish community. Many of the first members of our
community came from Panama and various islands
located in the Caribbean. The New York community today
consists of roughly seven congregations that are affiliated
with the International Israelite Board of Rabbis.[3]

There are families in Rabbi Funnye's congregation in Chicago,
as well as in other Israelite congregations, that have been practicing Judaism since the early part of the 1900s.[4] Their religious
lives move in parallel to the religious lives of white Jews, incorpo-
rating, as Jews have done for thousands of years, the cultural
practices of the society in which they live. In some mainly African
American synagogues, for example, more animated music,
including many instruments, may play a larger role in services
than in synagogues of European origin, and the congregants may
be livelier and more responsive to the rabbi, similar to some
African American gospel churches. Some refer to themselves as
"Israelites" or "Hebrews," distinguishing themselves from white
"Jews." They are, in every respect, deeply observant Jews, who
practice no other religion.

And yet, their legitimacy—the Jewishness of their blood and
therefore their ability to bear Jewish children—is placed under a
cloud of doubt by some Jews. Some Jewish institutions and their
representatives may be too quick to question the legitimacy of
Israelite communities because of race. Jews of color, no matter
how observant, do not "look Jewish" to most white Jews; a white
person who behaves as a Jew—or even simply claims to be a
Jew—is much less likely to be asked for proof of membership in
the Jewish community. More often than not, communities of black
Jews, even those with rigorous procedures of conversion and

ritual acceptance like Rabbi Funnye's Israelite community, must prove that they have real standards. While the ceremonies and rituals may be marginally different, this does not mean that they are illegitimate. Variation does not equal fraud.

The questions of the legitimacy of the Israelite community serve as a metaphor for the most fundamental and visceral struggles of Jewish identity. Jews, like all religious and ethnic groups, have boundaries. Those who would pass through the gates must fulfill certain requirements. How those boundaries are defined remains the most challenging question. Does one gain admittance through blood? Through practice? Who has the authority to determine legitimacy? Diverse Jews are not—and should not be— waiting for the approval of the "normative Jewish community." When do those who practiced Christianity in the past and have adopted Judaism become "accepted," and who are the arbiters of those processes? When race enters the picture, how do we delineate boundary concerns from a fear of outsiders, especially those of a different color? Boundaries are legitimate: practicing Christians, even "Judaic Christians"(Christian groups that use some Jewish symbols and ritual), are not Jews. Conversely, practicing Jews are not Christians. When race is involved, are we unable to tell the difference?

The other side of the "Who is a Jew?" discussion comes from the African and African American communities themselves. Rabbi Sholomo ben Levy, president of the International Israelite Board of Rabbis and rabbi of the Beth Elohim Hebrew Congregation in St. Albans, New York, explains the origin of the Jewish practices of African Americans in Harlem during the early part of the 20th century. He sees the origins of black Judaism in traditions and practices carried on from the African Jewish Diaspora and brought to the New World along with slavery. African Americans feel they did not convert to Judaism, but rather returned to their religious roots: "The possible origins of these Hebraic traditions [among blacks of Harlem] could be traced to West Africa where a number of tribes have customs so similar to Judaism that an ancient connection or maybe even descent from one of the 'ten Lost Tribes' is believed."[5]

An additional influence on the creation and philosophy of the Hebrew Israelite Community was Marcus Garvey, whose message of Black nationalism and pan-Africanism led Rabbis Ford and Matthew to make a connection between being black and being Jewish. The rabbis "reasoned that if many of the ancient Hebrews were black [as Garvey espoused], then Judaism was as much a part of their cultural and religious heritage as is Christianity. In their hearts and minds they were *not* converting to Judaism, they were reclaiming part of their legacy.[6] This fit very neatly with the Biblical prophecies that spoke of the Israelites being scattered all over the world, being carried in slave ships to distant lands, and of being forced to worship alien gods (Deuteronomy 28)."[7] In other words, some black nationalists believe that to be black is *de facto* to have Jewish blood.[8]

In addition to entire communities like the Israelites, there are racially and ethnically diverse Jewish individuals whose parents or grandparents were Jewish and who themselves may be secular or religious, Reconstructionist, Reform, Conservative, or Orthodox, partnered with another Jew or with a non-Jew. They are not affiliated with a specific racial community of Jews but rather are members, if they choose to affiliate at all, of mainstream congregations. In other words, they are just like the majority of American Jews, except that they are African American or Asian or Latino. They are the stealth diverse Jews, whose institutional legit- imacy stems from their forebears and whose Jewish identity is likely to be as conflicted or as strong as that of any other American Jew, with the added layer of race.

By Choice or by Destiny

For some racially and ethnically diverse Jews, the Jewish part of their identity comes to them not by birth but by choice, which carries with it its own set of challenges and opportunities. Rabbi Capers Funnye tells of a journalist who was writing a story about his congregation of African American Jews in Chicago. "[The writer] titled the story, 'Twice Cursed.' Twice cursed! 'You were cursed,' he said, 'because you were born black, and that that wasn't bad enough. You became a Jew! You're twice cursed.' Remember, this is a Jewish writer. I said, 'What kind of Jew are you? I am twice *blessed*, not twice cursed.' What I am is *who* I am, and it is a blessing *that* I am. And now what I have become has fulfilled me."

Rabbi Funnye's story is emblematic of the attitude many converts have to face from born Jews. Those who do not have to make a choice, who do not have to make an effort to join the Jewish people, often have little understanding of—and therefore little desire to reach out to—those who have undertaken the journey.

Jews-by-birth can be suspicious of Jews-by-choice. And when that Jew-by-choice is not white, the suspicion only grows. Yet, there has been an increase in the number of people who have chosen to convert to Judaism. In a time when the numbers game seems to be so present in the minds of many communal leaders, it is ironic that there be so much conflict about whether and how to embrace people who ask to join the Jewish community. Never mind that Jews-by-choice can help strengthen the Jewish population in countless ways, or that converts have always played a central role in Jewish history, some Jewish leaders fear that converts will harm the Jewish community.[1]

Some members of the Jewish community are resistant to converts because they fear that converts will "dilute" the Jewish community, taking away its distinguishing characteristics, particularly its ethnic and cultural traditions.[2] If the convert is not white, that fear is further compounded by the "foreignness" of introducing into the Jewish community a different race or ethnicity. If "Jews are white," as so many believe, then ethnically and racially diverse converts do not represent the growth of the Jewish community but rather the tumbling of the walls that kept the community safe from assimilation and dissolution. Some people question the allegiances of Jews-by-choice, wondering if they really have the best interests of the Jewish community at heart, or if they will damage the community from within. Ironically, for some non-observant Jews there is a (tacit) fear of and discomfort with the religiosity of converts, who as a group are often more observant than many existing members of the Jewish community. Converts often feel they need to be more religious to prove their legitimacy, particularly diverse converts.

Given all the institutional and personal barriers thrown up at those who knock on the guarded gates of the Jewish people, it is a wonder that anyone persists in getting through. Those who persevere and succeed in becoming Jews, usually do so out of faith, strength, and some personal need that can only be met through their conversion. For adults who convert to a new religion, there is either an *external* reason to explore a new religious practice, like marriage or partnership with someone of another faith, or an *internal* reason, such as a spiritual longing that is not being met by their current religious affiliation or practice.

Whatever their racial or ethnic background, Jews-by-choice tend to become Jewish through their own persistence. Potential Jews are often discouraged from pursuing conversion by the organized Jewish community. Even without the overlay of race and its visible differences, the gatekeepers make conversion unnecessarily difficult. In an earlier study, researchers called thirty congregations in the San Francisco Bay Area expressing an interest in converting to Judaism, and callers were told, variously, that they "didn't do that," or that "the rabbi is busy."[3]

These barriers are sometimes too formidable to overcome. Many individuals will live Jewish lives on their own for years before having the confidence to break through the obstacles that exist to keep out strangers, particularly strangers who look different from the majority. By the time diverse Jews are ready to convert, they often continue to search to find a community that is welcoming and positive. And then, even after formally joining the Jewish people, half the respondents (50%) to the Institute for Jewish & Community Research survey reported that they felt "less accepted in the Jewish community because I was not born Jewish."

> Given all the institutional and personal barriers thrown up at those who knock on the guarded gates of the Jewish people, it is a wonder that anyone persists in getting through.

There are barriers even for those who are too small to knock on the gates. There are a growing number of adopted children whose parents convert them to Judaism during infancy or early childhood. When Barbara, a white Reform Jew, sought a *mohel* for her infant son, recently adopted from Vietnam, she was told three times that he "did not *need* a *bris*, because he wasn't *really* Jewish, he was Asian." She eventually found another mohel to perform the ceremony.

Racism combined with homophobia forms an even more formidable barrier. David, a white Jewish man and his non-Jewish same-sex partner called an Orthodox mohel four times in an attempt to have a bris for their newborn black and Latino adopted son. When the mohel finally spoke with them, he refused to perform the bris unless authorized by the rabbi. "When I explained to the rabbi's wife why I needed to speak with him," David said, "she hung up the phone. I called back, and she again refused to put him on. We ended up finding a Conservative mohel who had been born in China and had converted as a young woman. She understood what we were up against."

Generally accepted rabbinic tradition endorses measures that discourage conversion. Some rabbis still follow the centuries-old tradition of turning away a would-be convert three times before engaging in a conversation about conversion.[4] Converts must prove their "sincerity" by their persistence. Rabbis can make conversion seem unappealing, asking questions such as why someone would want to burden themselves with the prejudice and discrimination historically heaped upon Jews. Additionally, rabbis often insist that potential converts adhere to more strict ritual observance than is practiced by many, if not most, of their own congregants.

In the Institute for Jewish & Community Research study, nearly half of the respondents (41%) who had converted spoke with more than one rabbi as part of their journey, because "some

> Rabbis often insist that potential converts adhere to more strict ritual observance than is practiced by many, if not most, of their own congregants.

rabbis were not very encouraging." Over a quarter of the converts (28%) felt that the rabbis had not been receptive because of their race. Rachel, a 48-year-old African American who had a Reform conversion when she was 29, had to convince the rabbi to allow her to continue. "The rabbi rejected my requests twice, but I am persistent. I didn't know that he was 'supposed' to do that. On the third attempt, he said, 'Why do you want to be a Jew? Don't you know that Jews are hated the world over?' I replied, 'Look at this face. Do I care? I know what hate is.' He stopped for a moment and thought about that as if it had never occurred to him. Then he said, 'We'll start right away.'"

Even among diverse Jews there are prejudices against conversion, including within the Sephardic community. Rabbi Manny Viñas explains that "according to Jewish law each community has a right to create laws for the community that it governs." Many of the Latino Jews who are part of Rabbi Viñas' Sephardic congregation are Anusim who converted or returned to Judaism. He explains that "the assumption made in many Near Eastern communities is the same as in Ashkenazi communities. Anyone with a darker complexion is assumed to be a convert. They will not bury a convert in the cemetery regardless of how long that person has participated with the community, or even if they personally saw that the person was totally observant."[5]

Acceptance should not be so difficult, according to Professor Ephraim Isaac:

> Bio-ethnic or racial superiority was not in the prophetic Jewish tradition, which considered Jewish "chosenness" strictly from the point of view of the responsibility for taking the Torah. Throughout history, proselytes were not only welcome but praised, among others by Rambam, as more heroic and praiseworthy than born Jews for voluntarily accepting the yoke of the Torah.[6]

Of course, people of all races do convert, and the experience can be welcoming. Clinton, an African American man, was initially treated rudely by one rabbi. The rabbi had been recommended by a friend, "and I called him, and I told him who I was and what my experience was and that I wanted to know if he would take some time to just give me some information, and he said yes. That I should come to a meeting and he would call me. So I contacted him again, but it just never manifested, and the phone calls were never returned either." Clinton was forgiving. "I think everybody is an individual. It depends. Not even what sect they are. I think it really depends on the rabbi, because since I've been going through the process [of conversion], I've met some

People of all races do convert, and the experience can be welcoming.

rabbis who are nice people. I think they're always really curious about what you're doing there, who you are, why you're there. Because I think that [my being black] might seem a little foreign to them. I know [a rabbi], and the first time I met

him he was taken aback a little. Like 'Oh, you're the guy I spoke to on the phone.' But after that it was Shabbat, he spent a little time talking to me, and he was cool. We got along well. The current rabbi I'm with now, I feel that he is a good rabbi, but I think he tries to get anybody to be a member of his congregation so that he can have a lot of families in his congregation. Getting one more family is always good, because it looks good for the rabbi." It is possible, then, that even when a rabbi and a community are genuinely open and welcoming, the history of rejection is so deeply ingrained, that newcomers may remain suspicious for a long time after they have entered that community.

Other people who convert feel that it is the tone with which they are treated, not actual Jewish law, that can be discouraging. "Why can't we look at it as strictly what it is?" asked Russ, an

African American man. "At least in the Conservative tradition, if you look at what happens, it is that you formalize this process through a judicial framework. For example, I've gone before the beit din. You have to look at the fact that this is a legal process. I look at it as more than just a simple, 'Now I am Jewish.' Like marriage. The formal process of marriage. It is not legal if you are living together."

Dana, also African American, agreed. "And it is also spiritual. There is a lot to learn, and there's a procedure. There's an order to it, and it is something new. I mean, this has gone on since the beginning of time that people have joined the faith and have had to meet certain criteria to be considered."

Once inside, people report feeling that the journey was worthwhile. Others report only positive experiences from the outset: their inquiries and the conversion process were met with enthusiasm and encouragement. Fred, an African American convert, said,

Other people who convert feel that it is the tone with which they are treated, not actual Jewish law, that can be discouraging.

"Not only does [the conversion process] teach discipline but there's been an order, a certain way for people to come within the religion since its existence. We just can't say, all right, I'm a Jew today, I'm a Moslem today, I'm a Rasta today, I'm a Christian the next day. It has to be something that somebody is really serious about, that is really heartfelt. And we do convert and become part of Judaism. We are probably super-Jews because we are probably more observant and know more about the liturgy than a lot of people who have been there all their life. We haven't gone through the drudgery of being forced to go to Hebrew school. We haven't been forced to go to High Holidays when we didn't want to. We made a conscious decision as adults to do something, and therefore we have a fervor that's not there [for many born Jews]."

Many of the people who come to Judaism without an external motivator arrive at the doors of a synagogue after a long, often arduous, and always deeply personal journey. For some, the journey takes them from church to church (or church to mosque) to synagogue. Even after converting to Judaism, many religious seekers continue their journey, flowing from Reform to Conservative to Orthodox congregations via multiple conversions. When they finally arrive at their final stop, many people report a sense of destiny fulfilled, of coming home without having known where home was located. "I'm not at all comfortable with the term 'Jew-by-choice'," said Richard, a mixed-race (African American and Native American) man who converted to Judaism. "I am a Jew-by-destiny. It is the only legitimate path that my soul could take."

> *"I'm not at all comfortable with the term 'Jew-by-choice.' I am a Jew-by-destiny. It is the only legitimate path that my soul could take."*

People who have switched religious affiliations multiple times are often unable to describe what they were seeking when they began their explorations. Some report an inchoate sense of dissatisfaction and a need for a spiritual center, a feeling that acts as the catalyst for their journey. Like Columbus looking for a new path to the East Indies, some religious seekers begin their quest without the intention of discovering for themselves a new world. Indeed, conversion to another religion is often far from their minds when they begin questioning themselves and their spiritual leaders about the meaning of their religious practices. It is the lack of satisfactory answers—the contradictions and inconsistencies from their clergy, their religious texts, and their communities—that sets them off on their journey of exploration, destination unknown.

Russ was initially raised with no religion. His African American father was Southern Baptist, his mother a Buddhist from Korea, where he was born. Russ was raised "with no religion in my life. If there was any real kind of spirituality or religion, it was from martial arts. [From there] I got into Buddhism and stuff like that. I joined the Navy for eight years. While I was in the Navy, I became a Christian, but I had questions. I always had questions. Why this? Why that? Why does it say here we eat anything, but over here it says, 'Don't eat pork'? And the answer was always, 'When Jesus Christ died on the cross, he said we don't have to do that anymore. We're free from all these things.' And there was always a conflict between what was written in the Greek in the New Testament and [written in] the Hebrew text. I didn't like the answers I was given, so that lasted for a year, and I quit."

After his forays into Buddhism and Christianity, Russ became more circumspect about his religious options. He had met a friend who was a Seventh Day Adventist, and "at that point, I decided that if I got into something, that I would research it very well. I wasn't going to take anybody's word for it. So I looked at it. I liked some of the things they believed in, and I didn't like some things. As time went on and I continued my research and my studies, I started having questions. All these questions. You never stop asking questions. So I said, if you keep the Jewish Sabbath, why don't you do Passover and Shavuot? And they went, 'Oh, well, Jesus died on the cross.' So I continued my research and looked at other things, and [my search] pointed me to Judaism. As a path in real life. The Seventh Day Adventism was a great stepping stone for me to get a slight look at Judaism." Finally, after another year and a half of study and research, including attending Introduction to Judaism, a course offered by the Union for Reform Judaism, Russ formally converted to Judaism with a Conservative beit din.

Prior to his discovery of Judaism, Russ did not have extended experience of Jews or Judaism. He was on a purely spiritual path that brought him to Judaism. For others, their journey towards Judaism began with an exploration of their racial or ethnic identity and ended up with their conversion to Judaism. Like Russ, Dana set out on a path of religious seeking and found herself unhappy with the answers she received from the various faiths she explored. Unlike Russ, though, Dana followed paths uniquely available to her as an African American. Those paths ran parallel to the world of Judaism and the Jewish people, close enough to Jewish thought and practice that Dana ended up becoming a Jew herself. It is not a coincidence that the two places where Dana came most into contact with Judaism were also the most black-identified: Rastafarianism and an Ethiopian church.

Dana was raised in a Southern Baptist family whose religious fervor began waning when her parents moved from the country to the city. Dana still felt a need for religion. As a girl in Baptist Sunday school, she "began to see a lot of different hypocrisy in Christianity. But when I got about college age and I started off on my own personal journey of seeking the faith of Hashem, I found this wealth of information, and I thought, wow, there really is a lot to this. With Christianity, you really just sit and listen, and there's not a lot of teaching. I found myself really inspired by the things that I was learning. It started opening itself up to me, and I found myself reading the Bible and finding more things in it. Buying books. Going to the library. Talking to people. Attending seminars. I did a little faith-hopping. I tried Islam, Bahá'í, Seventh Day Adventist. Each one brought me a little closer, because when I would start to try to study one of these faiths, I would run into that wall where there was no explanation. I kept being inquisitive; I had to move on. And my friends and family would say, 'What are you today? What are you this year?' They'd think it was funny, but I was just seeking."

Dana's seeking led her in a new direction: towards African-identified traditions with a Judaic component. They were not

Judaism, but they were oddly closer. "So I did a lot of studying of Rastafarianism, and they talk a lot about the tribe of Judah, and a lot of Hebrewism and Judaism are really wrapped up in that culture. But it is not tied in any way to what we say is Judaism, of course, but it is in there, and it will lead you. It led me further and further, it just kept pulling me, but I would have to know more. So then I wound up in the Ethiopian Christian Church. It's an ancient Christian church, orthodox Christian under the Coptic authority. It's really the link between Judaism and Christianity through Solomon and Sheba, so I thought, 'This is it! This is the epitome.' It was ritualistic. We didn't wear our shoes in the temple. The men and the women are separated. Just a lot of things that lifted it above the ordinary, as opposed to something that felt more mundane like in church. It gives you the liturgy and the service, it uses an ancient language, and it has the altar. Celebrates most of the High Holy Days. I thought, 'This is it. This is what I've been after.'"

For five years, Dana was a passionate member of the Ethiopian Orthodox Church, "but there were still these persistent questions. It wasn't enough. There was always this question of 'Where did this come from?' 'How did this get started?' And through studying and reading, including Ben Ami's book,[7] I started to think about Judaism. Everyone in the Orthodox Church balked at it. I talked with the priest for hours, and at the end he just couldn't answer my questions. So I was without a faith again for a few years. I wandered and read and studied on my own. And finally I mustered up the courage to walk into a synagogue." A few years later, she completed her Orthodox Jewish conversion.

Part of Dana's struggle to find her religious home was intellectual: her need to *understand* the origins and reasons behind certain practices. Another part of her struggle was spiritual: she embraced the strictures of worship of the Ethiopian Orthodox Church (and, later, her Orthodox synagogue), like separation of men and women. "Finding a faith that lifted up worship to a holy spiritual level was really fulfilling for me," she said. "It is part of the zeal with which we embrace our faith." Finally, part of her struggle was cultural. Both Rastafarianism and the Ethiopian Orthodox Church draw their identity and practices from a connection to Africa, to that part of Dana's identity that exists outside of her religious affiliation. Even more specifically, in both religions, Ethiopia is referred to as the *Promised Land*. Both traditions link themselves to Haile Selassie, the Ethiopian emperor who claimed to be the last descendant of Solomon and Sheba and who was known as "*Judah*, the Lion of Africa." Rastafarians, in the tradition of Judaic Christianity, follow dietary strictures similar to the laws of *kashrut*, including shunning pork and shellfish because they are "unclean."

> This link between historical Israel and historical Africa represents, for many black Jews in America and elsewhere, a cornerstone of their identity.

This link between historical Israel and historical Africa represents, for many black Jews in America and elsewhere, a cornerstone of their identity. While the religious practices of some groups range from Judaic Christianity to Exodus-tinged expressions of Black nationalism, others are more akin to Modern Orthodox and Conservative congregations. In Dana's case, while there were no African American synagogues in her community to join, her experiences with African-oriented spiritual traditions initially exposed her to Judaism—"Hebrewism", as the Rastafarians say—and paved the way towards her new identity as an African American Orthodox Jew.

For some people in the Institute for Jewish & Community Research study, childhood exposure to Jews helped form early impressions of Judaism and influenced their later decision to convert, even if the journey to Judaism took them down many other spiritual avenues first. This is particularly true for African Americans. White Jews and black Christians have long been in close contact through neighborhoods, schools, and employment. Some of these experiences have been contentious, others have been quite positive. For some African Americans, these interactions provided both an exposure and a first step on the path to becoming part of the Jewish people. Rebecca, like many African Americans growing up in the 1960s, had contact with Jews when she was young. She grew up in a small town in the southern Midwest; her mother was Baptist, her father an "atheist agnostic." She attended a Unitarian Church school and went regularly to the Unitarian Fellowship in town. "There were a lot of Jews in the Unitarian Fellowship, and there was a real respect for Judaism. Then my roommate in college was—and is—very involved in Modern Orthodoxy. She had invited me over for Shabbat dinners many Friday nights, and I loved it. That was what really got me interested."

"My exposure to Judaism after that was mixed. I was not really attracted to a lot of the restrictions. What I thought of as restrictions. I don't think of that the same way now, but a lot of the Orthodox observance of Shabbat and High Holy Days I wasn't attracted to at all. I wasn't attracted to walking in the snow to services and not turning on the lights. But I was attracted to the sense of family in the larger sense. And singing. And having something that came around every week where I could return to something. Still, I checked out a lot of things before I really committed to Judaism. I went to Quaker meetings when I lived in New Jersey. I would have people over on Friday nights for dinner. I didn't think of it or call it Shabbat, but there was something about that getting together that stayed with me. But I checked out a lot of other things. I checked out a Unitarian Fellowship in Philadelphia."

It was only after Rebecca was in a relationship with a non-observant Jew that she began attending services, insisting that they "at least have Friday night." (As often happens in interfaith relationships, her Jewish partner had little interest in Jewish religious observance and attended services with her only reluctantly.) Even with Shabbat dinners at home and regular attendance at services (which she continued long after the relationship had ended), she did not feel that she was on the path towards becoming a Jew. "If someone had said, 'You'll commit to a formal conversion to Judaism one day,' I don't think I would have agreed with that prediction."

Then, during a difficult period in her life, she met a teacher, a leader of the Jewish Renewal movement, and she "was blown away by the way that he taught and the kind of people who were attracted to his teaching. It was a much more diverse group of people in every way. There were people who were raised in traditional and observant homes. There were people who had no Jewish training but who identified as Jews. There were people who were Jews-by-choice. There were people from all over the world. There were Irish Jews. There were English Jews. There were Middle Eastern Jews. There was also diversity within his teaching. He would use melodies from different traditions or parts of the Jewish liturgy. I walked in, and they were singing something in Hebrew to the tune of 'Amazing Grace.' His teaching really got me involved, because one of the things that he taught was to make Judaism your own. Really examine what it is that you're saying. What's the meaning for you? How can you relate it to your life? How can you relate it to other people? Be innovative. Don't travel the old route. That was very important."

Rebecca and her family had positive interactions with white Jews long before she became Jewish herself. "In my nuclear family, there was great admiration for Jews and Judaism as being survivors. My father was in the military and was greatly admiring of the military of Israel. He loved it." Still, she didn't consider becoming Jewish herself until she was moved by the diversity of the Renewal movement.

For other people, secular exposure to Jews during their formative years marked the beginning of a conscious desire to become Jewish. Martin is one of several African American converts who said they felt an affinity for Judaism at an early age. "Intellectually, I've known I wanted to be a Jew probably since I was in high school. In the high school I went to, there were two kinds of people: there were Jews, and there were blacks. It was pretty much fifty-fifty. So, at a very early age, I was exposed to Jews. And in my past I was a Jehovah's Witness. I was born and raised as a Jehovah's Witness. In fact, in my childhood, we didn't celebrate Christmas and we didn't celebrate Easter, but we did celebrate Passover. So I had this thing in mind that that was the right way to go from the very, very beginning. I got rid of my interest in Jehovah's Witness in college, and I was nothing there. I was floating around having a great time just being. I dabbled with Zen [Buddhism] and anything else I was able. I had locked out a whole lot, and I didn't need religion. I was looking for spirituality in other areas. And then I got a little older and began to realize that I wasn't really being committed to anything, so I looked at a whole range of options and found out that what I should do was complete the circle. And what I mean by completing the circle is go back to my original interest in Judaism."

For all of the different paths that people may take that lead to becoming a Jew, common themes do emerge among their varied stories: Judaism is appealing because of its communal structure, its emphasis on celebration, and its dynamic theological tenets. For many people who choose to convert to Judaism, it is Jewish religious practice that most attracts them. Robert, a Latino man, was raised as a religious Christian. When he decided to convert to Judaism, he struggled with prayer. "As a Christian, I prayed well.

I needed a new way to pray like I needed a hole in the head. My knees would hit the floor before my feet would in the morning, but it seemed wrong to continue this as a Jew. But when praying while standing, I lost all connection with God. I tried many things, and finally I found tefillin. I used the *First Jewish Catalog* to figure it out. As I wrapped the strap around my arm, I could feel God's presence getting closer. It was a feeling of anticipation, like hearing the steps of an old friend coming up the walk. As I placed the head tefillin on, I stepped forward and said, 'Here I am, God, a Jew as you wish me to be.' Then I felt a rush of connection with God. That was when I knew it was going to work out okay. It has. No regrets. I am glad and proud to be a traditional Jew. I know it. I love it. I am it. I am a Jew as He wishes me to be."

Some people are swept towards Judaism as part of the larger trend in America towards fluidity of religious identity. As people search for religious roots, many non-Jews have found that Jewish religious practices and cultural traditions answer their longing for spiritual grounding. In addition to the much-publicized interest in Kabbalah among Hollywood celebrities, Jewish thought resonates among many people not raised within a Jewish household. For Francine, a 67-year-old Asian American woman, becoming Jewish at age 21 was "an evolutionary process. I love to read, and slowly I developed an appreciation for Judaism. My appreciation and awe started with my learning about the prophets and their ethical concepts and values. I have a sense of wonder every time I think of how they originated their ideas at a time when the peoples of the world practiced human sacrifice, made slaves out of human beings, and manifested so much cruelty. I also get the same feelings when I read the Torah and realize the humanistic ideas reflected, considering the prevailing ideas and ways of ancient people at the time. I am proud to identify myself as a Jew."

While Americans in general may find their way to Judaism along their own personal paths, there are certain elements of

Jewish tradition that are appealing to a particular ethnic or racial group. For example, many African Americans identify with the story of Exodus and the plight of the Hebrew slaves in the Torah. Indeed, some African Americans consider Christianity to be the religion of slavery and see Judaism as celebrating the transition from enslavement to freedom. A large number of African American Jews in our study felt that they were not converting to Judaism, but rather *reverting* to traditions and beliefs that had come out of Africa. James, a 35-year-old black man, traced the roots of African American Jews back to Moses. "He was not different from the Egyptians," James said. "You could see from everything in Egypt that the Egyptians were black. And Moses led the children of Israel out of Egypt. Being black and being Jewish is not something different. We do know where the tribes [of Israel] went. Tribes went into Europe; tribes went into Africa during the exile."

> *Judaism's emphasis on tradition and family has cultural resonance for some Asian Americans.*

Julie, an African American woman, agreed. Thinking about the dispersal of the tribes throughout Africa and her conversion to Judaism, she said, "People just need to understand that we are where we belong." So many black respondents to the Institute for Jewish & Community Research study expressed similar feelings about the affinity between being Jewish and being African American that it seems that, if the community were to welcome them, the number of black Jews in America could grow significantly.

Along the same lines, Judaism's emphasis on tradition and family has cultural resonance for some Asian Americans. May, a 32-year-old Asian American woman, found that her conversion helped her to feel connected to her non-Jewish family and her Asian heritage. "Being Jewish has had a profound positive effect on my life," she explained. "It has given me strength and hope, helped me open up, helped me to connect to others, [and] given me a community." At first, her family did not share her enthusiasm. "Initially my parents, especially my mother, reacted quite coldly to my decision. Surprisingly, however, after I formally became Jewish [at age 26], my Jewish identity has actually brought my parents and me closer. It provided me with a means to learn more about my Taiwanese/Asian heritage, culture and my ancestors. When practicing Jewish life cycle rituals and celebrating holidays, I have asked my parents about corresponding rituals and holidays in the Taiwanese culture. We have noted many similarities. In addition, the synagogue *yahrtzeit* list has provided me with a vehicle by which to ask my parents about family members who have passed away."

> *"Judaism is so tasty, it's such a holy life, it feels so good that my family hid a secret for 500 years that could have killed them."*

Among Latinos descended from Iberian Jews forced to convert under Spanish and Portuguese rule, there has been a growing movement to reclaim Judaism. For some, like Rabbi Viñas, the connection to Judaism was unbreakable: "Judaism is so good, it's so tasty, it's so delicious, it's such a wonderful life, it's such a holy life, it feels so good that my family hid a secret for 500 years that could have killed them."[8]

There is a long tradition of welcoming back Jews who were forced to convert. An Israeli website dedicated to the topic of Anusim explains that "in the past, when returning to Judaism, Anusim often immersed in a *mikveh* as part a return ceremony, and were neither discouraged [as potential converts often are] nor were they required to first study." The following special prayer was composed by Rabbi Solomon ben Simeon Duran in the 15th century for such an occasion:

Our God and God of our Fathers, bring success to your servant [returnee's name supplied here] and bestow your grace upon him. Just as you have moved his heart to return in complete repentance before you, so may you plant in his heart love and fear of you. Open his heart to your Torah and guide him in the path of your commandments that he may find grace in your eyes. So may it be, and let us say Amen.[9]

Some contemporary Latinos who wish to return to Judaism feel resentful that they are being asked to "convert" to a faith that their ancestors did not choose to leave behind, or, in many cases, to a set of traditions that their families have secretly maintained, usually in some attenuated form, for centuries. The same website states that "Hispanics whose families are aware of Jewish descent and who wish to be accepted as part of a normative Jewish community face difficulties. Without conversion or formal return, they often find themselves marginalized in the synagogue or temple, unable to marry in the synagogue, or unable to settle permanently in Israel."[10]

For George, the idea of conversion itself is problematic. "I was raised a Catholic," he said. "My father is Italian and Catholic. My mother is Portuguese and Spanish and 'Catholic.' [I] put 'Catholic' in quotes because six years ago I walked into the Portuguese synagogue in Amsterdam, and I discovered a plaque by the *bima* in front that has names going back to the 1600s, people who supported the building of the temple, and my mother's last name was written there. I met some people in the temple who told me that it was a Jewish name. I had an uncle who was always saying he wouldn't go to church because he was a 'born-again Jew,' which tickled me because I had never heard of that kind of confirmation. When he passed away, I found a picture of him sitting on a canoe with a Star of David on it that nobody could explain or wanted to discuss. So I was inspired by that experience to look into this and find out what my real heritage was."

What he discovered was that his family had lived in Spain until the Edict of Expulsion of 1492. While many Jews fled to Morocco, Italy, and the Ottoman Empire, more than half went to neighboring Portugal, including his mother's family. Life in Portugal was intermittently difficult for Jews, but the royal family allowed them to stay because they valued Jews both for their financial contributions and for their skill in metallurgy for the ongoing wars against the Moors. Then, in 1497, when King Manoel wanted to solidify his tenuous claim to the Portuguese throne by marrying the daughter of the Catholic King and Queen of Spain, Fernando and Isabel, he made his offer of matrimony more attractive by cleansing his country of Jews, just as his neighbors had done recently. George explains the fate of his mother's family: "So my family had water thrown at them as crowds of Jews did at that time. They immediately became Catholic. And my family stayed in Lisbon until about 1540, when they left to go to Holland because they could practice in Holland openly. But you couldn't go to Holland, so they went to Madeira off the coast of Morocco, and they lived there until 1895. And then my great-grandfather signed a contract to go to Hawaii to cut sugarcane for three years. And they arrived with hundreds of other Portuguese, thousands ultimately. They were all Jews. They had left Madeira and cut sugar for three years, and then they immigrated to this country. In doing genealogical research, I found that my family is very typical [of Portuguese crypto-Jews], because they married within the fold. On my mother's side cousins married cousins for 500 years, because they didn't want to bring anybody else in to find out what their secret was. And even my mother, who swore she had no knowledge of being Jewish, did things like clean the house on Friday afternoon so she could be ready for the weekend. And in Portugal, my family's experience was that you had to eat pork. If you didn't eat pork, you were Judaized, and if you were Judaized, you could be put to the planks. So the Portuguese Jews found that if they soaked pork in vinegar that it would make it 'kosher' and they could eat it. Around Passover, they made *malasadas*, which means in Portuguese, 'it won't rise.' So they would make these Easter treats of unleavened bread. The frightening thing for me in all of this is that I always felt not Catholic. But I really felt ripped off by the Inquisition."

Still, even with 500 years of Catholicism in his family, once he discovered that his mother's family was originally Jewish, he did not feel the need to convert. "[T]he chief Sephardic rabbi in Jerusalem, [Mordechai Eliahu, stated that] people like myself don't have to convert, that we're already Jews. That's not accepted by most congregations. I haven't converted, but I have always felt more leaning towards—because I've had Jewish friends—the Jewish religion than I did with Catholicism. I don't like having a third party to go talk to God. So I've studied Judaism a bit, and there are things I like about it. And I feel Jewish, but I haven't done anything formal. Maybe as I get older. They say as you get older, you start studying for the final exam. And you start getting more religious."

> For those Latinos who have undergone conversion, the experience of publicly becoming a Jew means finding an answer to familial and spiritual longings for which they previously had no name.

George is not alone. In addition to Rabbi Eliahu, some scholars and religious leaders, including the (Orthodox) Chicago Rabbinical Council, have been advocating an adoption of a "return" ceremony rather than a formal conversion as a way of increasing the number of Latinos who wish to become (once more) a part of the Jewish community.[11]

For those Latinos who *have* undergone conversion, the experience of publicly becoming a Jew means finding an answer to familial and spiritual longings for which they previously had no name. Joe was raised Catholic. He knew that his family had originally come from Italy, Portugal, and Spain, but knew little more about them. As an adult, he converted to Judaism for spiritual reasons. It was only after his conversion that he traced his family history to discover that they were Conversos. He describes the moment of discovering that his ancestors had been Jews as "frightening," a feeling that gave way to anger at the Inquisition, a sense, like George, that he had been cheated by history.

Jaime, born and raised Catholic in a Mexican family, always felt that there was something Jewish about his family, but he did not know why he felt that way. "There was a mystery there," he said. "My parents had a way of being, I don't know, like not eating pork." For four years, Jaime lived in New York. "And I was interested in the Jewish religion, apart from the fact that I was researching my family tree. After that I went to Mexico to see my parents. It was at Christmas time that I got together with my family. I met an aunt, and she told me, you know you have Jewish family in New York. I didn't know about that. So she put me in touch with that part of my family." Jaime went to see this family, and when his aunt in New York City opened the door to her apartment, "it was an atmosphere of Sephardic things like spices and candles. I was kind of living a dream. For me it was just so much. So from that particular experience, I started looking for things and started researching and finally found that I have a relative that dates back to the 16th century on my father's side. Where my people come from is Spain. Sephardic." The irony is that Jaime had already converted to Judaism when he discovered that his family had always been Jewish.

> If the Jewish community persists with the notion that you are either with us or against us, some number of Jews will simply opt out, and take their spouses and their children with them.

Roberta, a 57-year-old descendant of Conversos, converted in a Reform ceremony that had profound implications. The simple act of "holding the Torah and speaking, praying the blessings in public after so many hundreds of years of not being able to be a Jew in public—openly" was the most moving part of her conversion experience. There are others like Roberta, some who have already converted, others who are only now recognizing their affinity for Judaism.

A number of scholars and leaders seem unaware of the potential of (re)opening the gates to once and future Jews like Roberta and Jaime. The numbers of the descendants of the Jews who fled, hid, or were converted during and after the Inquisition and expulsion are huge. Tens of millions of people in Latin America, the American Southwest, and Iberian Peninsula have some Jewish ancestry. The potential for Jewish population growth is enormous.

> *Ultimately, can a community fearful for its own long-term survival afford to turn away those who would seek to enrich and strengthen it, no matter their origins?*

Still, many argue that to sustain the Jewish community, efforts must be focused on the existing members and particular energy devoted to the prevention of religious intermarriage. Some believe that the non-Jewish spouse should be encouraged to convert only when efforts against intermarriage have failed.[12] Other analysts claim that conversion does not ultimately sustain the Jewish community, because the children of converts may not choose to be Jews.[13] While it is true that some children of converts do not become or remain Jewish, this should be seen as a clear sign that the Jewish community should be more welcoming to converts— and thus create more incentive for their children to be Jewish— rather than as an indication that intermarriage must be stopped (a doomed effort, certainly, in our multicultural society).

Additionally, even if some children of converts do not become or remain Jewish, is this a real reason to discourage conversion? What about the contributions to the Jewish community of the converts themselves? Furthermore, there is no guarantee that children of born Jews will choose to continue to be Jewish when they become adults.[14]

All these add up to conversion being foreboding rather than warm and welcoming. Ultimately the effect of our current approach to conversion—that conversion should be allowed only as a last resort—is to keep out potentially strong and vibrant new Jews and also to drive existing Jews away, further diminishing the population If the Jewish community persists with the notion that you are either with us or against us, some number of Jews will simply opt out, and take their spouses and their children with them.

> Abraham, Rachel, and Ruth were all converts. Acceptance, not exclusion, has been our tradition.

The dichotomy of "inside the tent" versus "outside the tent" does not capture the reality of life. Jewish identity and behavior exist along a continuum of feeling, practice and involvement. An individual's connection to Judaism, whether born Jewish or some other religion, changes over time. Opportunities for encouraging and helping each person to be welcomed and included, or shunned and ignored, take place multiple times as someone moves along their life path. At each juncture, the Jewish community needs to accept people where they are, encouraging them for what they do at that point, or how far they have come, and the ways they are involved with Judaism. Focusing on what someone does not do, what they do not know or their incompleteness as Jews is a self-fulfilling prophesy of decline.

Ultimately, can a community fearful for its own long-term survival afford to turn away those who would seek to enrich and strengthen it, no matter their origins? Historically, religious communities that have insulated themselves against the influx of outsiders have either not been able to sustain themselves (e.g., the Shakers, with only a handful of extant members) or have consigned themselves, like the Druze (also known as Mowahhidoon), to an unclear long-term future, since their sustainability is entirely dependent on their birthrate.

Some efforts are being made to encourage conversion.[15] These include educational programs for potential converts and training for individuals to help mentor converts. There are the efforts of individual synagogues, as well as institutional efforts like Neal Weinberg's *Introduction to Judaism* courses at the University of Judaism, *The Conversion to Judaism Resource Center* led by Rabbi Lawrence Epstein, and an online *Introduction to Judaism* course offered by Rabbi Celso Cukierkorn, intended for people who are distant from a Jewish community or from access to a rabbi who may work towards conversion.[16]

The potential to (re) open the gates of the Jewish community to these once and future Jews is enormous. If the gates *are* open, it is possible that Judaism will look far more African, Asian, and Latino fifty years from now, just as America as a whole will look. After all, Abraham, Rachel, and Ruth were all converts (and none was European either). Acceptance, not exclusion, has been the Jewish tradition.

And for Those Too Young to Ask: Transracial Adoption

Jews today adopt at approximately the same rates as non-Jews. The trend of cross-cultural adoption started in force after the Korean War, when Korean orphans were brought into the United States. The number of transcultural adoptions remained relatively small until the 1980s, when the number of white children who were available for adoption dropped significantly, the result of wider use of birth control, higher rates of abortion, and better education.[1] In 2001, Americans officially adopted 19,000 children from abroad, three times more than in 1992.[2] At the same time, more than 110,000 foster children were available for adoption in the United States The majority (59%) of these were African American, 29% were white, and 10% Latino.[3]

A study of Jewish adoptive families by Howard Alstein of the University of Maryland showed that the parents are largely well-educated and upper-middle class.[4] With the continuing shortage of healthy white babies for adoption in the United States, many of these parents, like non-Jewish parents, adopt from outside the country, mostly from China, Korea, and Latin America.[5] According to Stars of David, a non-profit support and information network for Jewish and interfaith adoptive families, approximately 25% of Jewish families that adopt bring home children born outside of the

United States.[6] In 2001, the federal government issued China the highest number of visas for adoption from abroad. Because of China's one-child policy and the bias toward having male children, 95% of children available for adoption from China are girls.[7] Like white non-Jews, white Jews prefer to adopt an overseas Asian child over a domestic African American child. Some have attributed this tendency to society's higher level of racism against African Americans. There is no doubt that for many parents their preference is due to their fear of creating what they believe will be more difficulties in their (adopted) children's lives. Some families simply are not equipped to handle the complexities inherent in transracial adoptions.

> *Sadly, in this ugly racial construct, African American boys are at the bottom of the adoption food chain.*

The growing number of Jewish families choosing to adopt can be attributed, in part, to the high rate of infertility among Jewish women. More women are waiting longer to have children, choosing instead to pursue careers first. As a result, many women with higher levels of education and in higher socio-economic brackets find themselves unable to conceive when they do decide to begin a family. Additionally, the changing social and legal climate in some parts of the United States has enabled traditionally "marginalized" families and individuals within the Jewish community, as well as within the general population, to adopt children. This includes gay- and lesbian-headed families, as well as single and older adults. With the number of healthy white infants available for adoption in the United States dropping every year, the choices available to older and non-traditional families move down the (unspoken) chain of desirability to include children traditionally considered second or even third tier in the rarefied world of adoption. Sadly, in this ugly racial construct, African American boys are at the bottom of the adoption food chain.

For observant Jews, adoption of a child can be a tricky business. While the Torah and Talmud contain multiple, heart-warming stories of adoption, foster parenting, and other "honorary" parent-child relationships (think Esther and Mordechai; Moses and Pharaoh's daughter, Batiah; King David's wife Michal and her sister's five sons, and so on), Jewish law, with its strict emphasis on bloodlines, makes no *legal* accommodations for these relationships.

In fact, there was no word for "adoption" in biblical Hebrew. Modern Hebrew uses the word *ametz*, "to strengthen," a reference to the verse from Psalm 80: "be mindful of this vine…which Thy right hand *has planted* and the branch that Thou *madest strong* for Thyself." This word and this verse imply the honor attributed to adoption; many see it as a mitzvah, as adoptive parents take on the responsibility of raising a child whose life's journey is radically different from what it would have been had he or she not been placed for adoption, especially adoption by a Jewish family.[8]

Civil law, of course, creates a bond between adoptive parents and their children that is legally indistinguishable from that between biological parents and children, including the issuance of a new birth certificate with the adoptive parents' names replacing those of the birthparents. But, according to Rabbi Michael Gold, adoptive father and author of *And Hannah Wept; Infertility, Adoption, and the Jewish Couple,* no matter who raises a child (and, presumably, regardless of civil law), that child will always carry with him or her an indelible identity based on blood.

This emphasis on bloodlines has serious consequences for adoption in Jewish law. For example, the status of the birth mother as Jew or gentile at the moment of birth establishes the identity of the child as Jewish or gentile. If

the mother is Jewish, then the father's tribal status as a
Kohen, Levi, or Yisrael decides the child's tribe. If a Jewish
woman became pregnant as a result of adultery or incest,
the child would take on the status of a *mamzer*, and
traditional Jewish law would forbid such a person from
marrying a Jew of legitimate birth.[9]

For traditional Jews worried about the Jewish status of their
child, the solution is to adopt a child whose birthparents are *not*
Jewish, and then to have that child undergo an Orthodox conversion as soon as possible. At that point, the problem of bloodlines
seems to fade. According to Rabbi Gold, "*Halakhically* there is no
problem; Judaism is not a race, and such a child, if properly
converted, is fully Jewish."[10] Fully Jewish, yes, but without the full
rights and privileges that would have been accorded a birth child,
since the adoptive father's Jewish tribal affiliation does not pass to
his adopted child. If the father is a Kohan or Levi, for example,
that identification is forbidden to an adopted child. According to
halakha, blood still matters.

If the child is not white, the problem of identity continues to
be complicated. Just as "in Judaism, personal status [as a born
Jew] is based on bloodlines and lineage, [and] no legal procedure
or court decree can erase that [Jewish] identity,"[11] so it is with the
child's racial identity. An adopted child of color converted to
Judaism remains a child of color, both in his or her own eyes and
in the eyes of the world. Several adoptive parents in our study
said that members of their community, upon seeing their non-
white adopted children for the first time, asked, "Are you going to
raise them Jewish?" One quick-thinking mother of a Chinese-born
girl responded, "No, we thought we would raise her Christian ...
This is a Jewish family. What other religion would we raise her
in?" She conceded that she may have been asked the question in
part because her daughter was adopted rather than *solely* because
she was from China, but the result is the same: given the halakhic
emphasis on bloodlines (and despite halakhic insistence that a

convert is fully a Jew), many mainstream Jews struggle to "see" adopted children as real Jews. The question of being *seen* is both figurative and literal (visual). Many Jews hold a mental image of what a Jew looks like, particularly in the United States, and that image may not include ethnically and racially diverse Jews (nor, for that matter, blonde and blue-eyed Nordic types). As a result, the appearance of ethnically and racially diverse adopted children in the seats of synagogues and Jewish day schools leads to an uncomfortable question: *What do Jews look like in America?*

For many people, the struggle for legitimacy begins when the children are tiny. When Sue and her then-husband, both white, adopted their son, Jonathan, from Korea in 1982, they were living in a mid-sized city in the South, "not a good place for an inter-racial family. Even the Jewish community was not open to this [half-black, half-Korean] baby. One week after Jonathan arrived, we went to Shabbat services. The first person to see us told us that, of course, he could never attend the Jewish day school. Not that they were happy that a nice couple had adopted a baby, or that a baby had found a nice home. Some people, especially the cantor and the rabbi of our congregation, were thrilled for us, but the community as a whole was not welcoming. We convinced the local mohel to circumcise the baby, although we had to 'prove' that we were committed and practicing Jews. He would not circumcise simply for conversion." When Jonathan was still a toddler, Sue separated from her husband and moved to the Midwest to be closer to her family.

Although she blamed the South in part for her son's struggles, her home in the Midwest did not prove to be more accepting. "Jonathan has suffered prejudice on a daily basis. He wears his Judaism, his adoptive status, and his heart on his sleeve, and they all get hurt. When Jonathan was four, an older child at day care sat on him until he cried because he didn't believe in Santa Claus. He attended religious school starting at age four. While there were no other black Koreans in our Jewish community, he somehow managed to fit in and charm everyone. His biggest problem with Sunday school came each year when Martin Luther King's birthday was celebrated. The religious school children would gather for an all-school assembly, something relevant to the national observance, but as the only black child in the building, even in the community, Jonathan felt singled out. Each year when I picked him up on that Sunday, he would come out of school in tears, even as a teenager. And yet, Jonathan is proud of his Judaism. He celebrated his bar mitzvah, attended religious school through confirmation, visited Israel with other Jewish teens, and volunteered to be an assistant teacher in religious school through high school graduation." Now that Jonathan is in college, "he continues to socialize with everyone. Race and religion are big topics of conversation, but he gets along with everyone."

For people who navigate multiple identities, "getting along with everyone" helps avoid being pigeonholed into any one ethnic or racial grouping.

For people who navigate multiple identities, "getting along with everyone" helps avoid being pigeonholed into any one ethnic or racial grouping. (Think of Sasha, whose story is told at the beginning of this book). In 1982, Sue and her husband were more unusual as parents (of any religion) adopting children of a different race. Now, as the number of healthy white infants available for adoption drops, transracial adoptions are becoming increasingly common. The majority of the adopted children of color being raised Jewish are still too young to form romantic relationships, but their parents, like Sue, are concerned how they will be received in the Jewish community as potential partners for other Jews. With so many identities tugging at their sleeves, some of these children may ultimately choose to reject the one identity that has never fully accepted them: being Jewish. When they are old enough to date, what will be the more important factor in determining their desirability (or undesirability) as romantic partners in the eyes of other Jews, their race or their religion? Which card trumps the other? Some adoptive parents try to help their children maintain a connection to all their available identities so that the children have a stronger foundation upon which to base their adult selves. Elaine, the white Jewish mother of two adopted Guatemalan children, describes the challenge as "issues of continuity, though not because our kids look different or because they (still) have Hispanic names. In many ways we have tried to validate their original Mayan heritage, but because they were not born Jewish, then the question arises, do we (and *how* do we) validate their non-Jewish (Christian) religious past? In other words, there are huge issues of multiple identities. What happens when they clash? Which one takes precedence? What role do we as parents have in validating or sorting these out?"

> *Since transracial adoption is becoming more common within the United States in general and specifically within the Jewish community, synagogues and other Jewish institutions are becoming more welcoming, and that welcome seems increasingly genuine.*

The picture for Elaine and other families like hers is increasingly less bleak. Since transracial adoption is becoming more common within the United States in general and specifically within the Jewish community, synagogues and other Jewish institutions are becoming more welcoming, and that welcome seems increasingly genuine. That is to say, as Jewish families change and the number of adopted Jewish children of color increases, Jewish institutions are slowly changing with them. For many families, this outreach towards all kinds of families feels less like a liberal tipping of the hat towards some abstract concept or mission statement seeking "diversity" and more a heartfelt desire to keep the Jewish community strong, whatever the tone of its skin. When Barbara's son entered kindergarten at a Jewish day school with "very little diversity," she worried that he "would feel like an outsider, not really 'Jewish.'"

Instead, she has found that the school "has gone out of its way to incorporate my son's Vietnamese heritage into the school curriculum. On their own, no suggestions coming from me, his kindergarten teachers developed a whole lesson plan around Tet—the Vietnamese New Year—and the Vietnamese people. The children learned the similarities in meaning between Tet and Rosh Hashonah. And they made their own costumes for a dragon parade on Tet that went through the school, the synagogue, and the Jewish Community Center. The school made this a standard part of their curriculum for every year, as they have done with other ethnic traditions as well. As a result, my son thinks that it is perfectly natural to be American and Vietnamese, Asian and Jewish. My concerns are for his future exposure to environments not as open as this one."

Her concerns have deep roots. Prejudice is a blight, not to be tolerated anywhere in America and certainly not within the Jewish community. The history of the Jews as an oppressed people, plus the expectation that a religious community should be welcoming and supportive, leave little room for the reality of prejudice that sometimes exists even within the walls of synagogues, community centers, and day schools. Despite official policies to the contrary, Jewish children of color sometimes face difficult and often painful journeys to adulthood as they strive to be seen as desirable members of the community. And when other Jews demonstrate their lack of acceptance—whether it be quiet or blatant—the entire community is debased. On the other hand, as the demographic composition of the Jewish community continues to change, more institutions are learning to be more accepting. Some adopted children have overwhelmingly positive experiences in Jewish day schools and other Jewish institutions.

Patches of Color,
Patches of White

Ahavas Sholom, a small Conservative synagogue in Newark, New Jersey, was languishing. Most of the eighty or so members of the congregation were elderly Ashkenazi Jews who could not ensure the shul's long-term survival. Then, in the early 1990s, the faces in the synagogue began to change, becoming younger, less familiar, and ... darker. Now, "the synagogue is beginning to offer a view of the mosaic that is Judaism today. In addition to recent Russian immigrants, there are Persian Jews, Brazilian Jews, and African American Jews [...], according to [Rabbi Arthur] Vernon. 'It's a microcosm of the contemporary Jewish world.'"[1] More specifically, Ahavas Sholom's journey is a reflection of the path the American Jewish population must take not only to survive, as this small New Jersey congregation has done, but to thrive into coming generations. Without a purposeful effort to welcome, encourage, and build communities of Jews of all kinds, the American Jewish community will find itself increasingly attenuated, surviving, perhaps, but without the vibrancy needed to grow stronger (except for the remaining Orthodox communities).

The demographic shift at Ahavas Sholom took place without a concerted effort on the part of the congregation's leadership, but the larger Jewish world cannot rely on serendipity for its future. Jewish fear of those perceived as strangers seems to grow even more acute when the "stranger" appears inside the walls of Jewish institutions. Rabbi Capers Funnye tells this story: A middle-aged black man walks into a synagogue on Saturday morning. He proceeds down the aisle and takes a seat near the front of the all-white congregation. He removes his tallit from its velvet bag and places it around his shoulders, adjusting his *yarmulke* on his head. As the service begins, he reads from his *siddur* in a deep, resonant Hebrew. When the cantor chants from the Torah, he nods his head knowingly. Finally, when the service has ended and the congregants have gathered for the Oneg Shabbat, the man who had been seated behind him during the service approaches.

> *Despite the growing number of diverse Jews and changing racial attitudes in America, racially and ethnically diverse Jews are not on the radar screen of the majority white Jewish community.*

"Excuse me," he says. "May I ask you a personal question?"

The black man nods.

"Are you Jewish?"

Funny, if it weren't true.

Despite the growing number of diverse Jews and changing racial attitudes in America, for the most part, racially and ethnically diverse Jews are not on the radar screen of the majority white Jewish community. That is not to say that they are invisible. Indeed, when a person of color attends a Jewish event, he or she is likely to feel all too visible. Almost half of the respondents (45%) to the Institute for Jewish & Community Research survey reported often or sometimes having anti-minority experiences within the Jewish community. Most of those who have "often or sometimes" had negative racial experiences were either Jewish families of color by conversion (50%) or by birth/partnership (54%). (See Figure 6.) Adoptive families of color fare somewhat better: only 34% reported frequent negative racial experiences. Of course, those families tend to be headed by white parents.

"My husband, who is African, our son, and I went to the annual Jewish community picnic," relates Joan, a white Jewish woman living in the Midwest. "This was before we knew many Jewish community people here. We received (especially my husband) many stares that felt invasive and curious, but when we met their glances, they always looked away as if embarrassed and never once responded with a smile or acknowledgement. We felt like oddballs, and no one came up to introduce themselves or made any effort at inclusiveness. I've never been able to get my husband to attend Jewish community events since then, unless they involve our kids."

Others report similar experiences. More than one-third (37%) of survey respondents "strongly" or "somewhat" agreed that they do not feel comfortable in a predominantly white synagogue because of their race. Skin tone seemed to be a factor in how comfortable a family or an individual felt in a predominantly

Figure 6
How often have you or your family experienced anti-minority attitudes in the Jewish community?

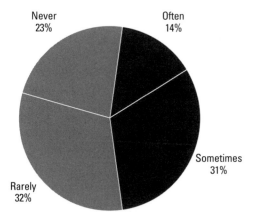

Source: *Survey of Racially & Ethnically Diverse Jews in the United States*, Institute for Jewish & Community Research, 2001.

white synagogue. Hank, a 60-year-old mixed-race Jew from Los Angeles, found that he could "pass" without much conversation. "I find that I have not been subject to a lot of discrimination," he said. "The main reason is that I'm fair-skinned, with African, American Indian, and European ancestry. I do not volunteer my 'race.'"

It is not surprising that some Asian American Jews received a similar kind of welcome from white Jews: different, but not always benign. Terri is the mother to two adopted Asian American girls. She has "rarely experienced [anti-minority prejudice] personally, and the Jewish people I know are very pro-Asian, but I certainly know many Jews who are biased against blacks and Latinos." To be "very pro-Asian" is itself a form of racism: blacks are threatening, Asians are not. Indeed, Devorah, another adoptive mother of a girl from China, found the pro-Asian sentiments of her Jewish community unsettling. She regularly heard stereotypes about her daughter disguised as compliments: "She's so good in math!" "She's so smart!" And, the clincher: "She's as pretty as a China doll!" With each "compliment," Devorah felt her daughter separated further from the Jewish mainstream.

Reggie does not have such an easy time. He's 27, a mixed-race (black/white) Jew in the San Francisco Bay Area. He wears his hair in dreadlocks and does not look like the majority of the Jews around him. Every time he attends services, he receives strange looks from the mainly white congregation, and he regularly feels rejected based on his African American appearance alone.

Since the most persistently malignant racial divide in America is between blacks and whites, it should come as no surprise that racial politics in America reach, if not their full expression, then at least a strong showing within the American Jewish community. What does it mean, for example, that the Israelite Board of Rabbis currently consists entirely of African Americans? For many in the Israelite community, their identity as Jews is inextricably linked to being black. What would happen to that identity if those of other races were encouraged to join? When the question is raised of accepting non-African American students at the all-black Israelite Rabbinical Academy in New York, some rabbis and other African American leaders may resist, fearful that the unique history of the institution would be compromised. Such fear is common among minority groups: if the majority is allowed in, will they co-opt the smaller groups' values, traditions, and principles? Yet, how can a minority group seek inclusion in the larger group if they themselves are proponents of separation? The paradox runs in both directions.

A website for black Jews introduces readers to the Israelite Board of Rabbis with the following message:

> Welcome to this place of meeting, sharing, and learning. While everyone is free to read the information contained on these and participate in the discussions that take place here, this site was specifically created as a gateway for people of color who wish to connect with others who share their faith and can identify with their experiences. If you are a friend, enter and explore. We greet you with Shalom![2]

Exclusion of others both creates a sense of belonging for those who are "in" ("connect with others who share their faith and can identify with their experiences") and separates the group from the larger community ("this site was specifically created [...] for people of color").

Clearly, the Israelite community must have a place in which they feel respected and represented. What does that mean, then, for their relationship to the larger Jewish community? Of course, the question itself presupposes that members of the Israelite community wish to be part of the larger community, which is not necessarily true for all members. But if they are to be accepted as part of the Jewish people—and many of their leaders have indicated by both deed and word that they do consider themselves part of the larger Jewish people—what can all the affected communities, both large and small, do to facilitate that desire?

Some leaders are able to bridge the gap and navigate multiple communities. For, example, Rabbi Funnye describes his congregation as "Conservadox." He is a member of the Chicago Board of Rabbis and a visible and important leader of the Jewish community, both in Chicago and at a national level. He maintains a deep affiliation with his own congregation in Chicago and with the Israelite community around the country, plus he maintains strong relationships with all branches of Judaism as well as with mosques and churches of many denominations.

There is no single "community of color" for all diverse Jews.

While there is no single "community of color" for all diverse Jews, cultural affiliations can help diverse Jews feel comfortable within the Jewish community. Latino Jews sometimes find comfort in Sephardic congregations, where people may look a little more like them and share some common historical and cultural references. Even for those Jews who do not consider themselves Anusim, the Spanish flavor and the symbolically shared heritage of a Sephardic community feel more comfortable than an Ashkenazi synagogue. Physical markers of difference are less noticeable than in non-Sephardic settings, culinary traditions are more familiar, plus Sephardic communities already exist outside the mainstream and therefore may be more compassionate about individuals seeking a Jewish home that is not Ashkenazi. Dina, herself a Sephardic Jew, has an adopted Latina daughter, "who stands out at services [in an Ashkenazi synagogue.] In contrast, reception is great at [my] Sephardic minyan." Additionally, some African American Jews report feeling more comfortable in Sephardic settings than in

mainly Ashkenazi institutions. Some African American Jews call
themselves Sephardic and follow Sephardic practices, a choice that
signifies the extent to which "Ashkenazi" means "white" to many
diverse Jews. But even then, the match is not perfect.

Rabbi Manny Viñas cautions against the mistake of assuming
that one community is universally welcoming to diverse Jews
while another is not. "I wish that the problem of non-acceptance
were confined to the Ashkenazim or to one community alone.
Unfortunately, this is not true at all. Many people assume that
Sephardim are more accepting of converts or of people of color.

This is also not true. Sephardim
have been cast into the minority
status by the larger Jewish community in the United States, but that
has not made them more accepting
of other peoples who are also cast
into the 'minority' social structure.
Acceptance levels vary from
community to community in both
the Ashkenazi and Sephardic
communities. To create unity in the
Jewish people we must accept each
other's differences with love and a lot of patience. This love and
patience needs to come from all sides, including from the
newcomers."[3]

> *"To create unity in the Jewish people we must accept each other's differences with love and a lot of patience. This love and patience needs to come from all sides, including from the newcomers."*

Whatever their paths to Judaism, many racially and ethnically
diverse Jews find entrance into mainstream Jewish communal and
institutional life difficult. Indeed, in the Institute for Jewish &
Community Research survey, over 85% of the respondents agreed
that "people of color have a difficult time fitting into the Jewish
community because they look different from the majority of Jews
in America." The group that felt this most strongly was diverse
Jews by birth (95%). Still, most diverse Jews belong to at least one

Jewish organization. In the Institute study of racially and ethnic-
ally diverse Jews, 58% of the respondents reported belonging to at
least one Jewish organization or group besides a synagogue. Many
of those groups were political or cultural, including the local
Jewish federation, Jewish community centers, Jewish National
Fund, Joint Distribution Committee, Jewish day schools, AIPAC
(American Israel Public Affairs Committee), Rabbis for Human
Rights, Americans for Peace Now, ARZA (Association of Reform
Zionists of America), Hadassah, Hillel, and others. The membership of many of these organizations has traditionally been white,
with the exception of Jewish community centers, where the
athletic or health facilities have always attracted a wider range of
people from the surrounding community.

However, the experience is not always positive. Michael is a
35-year-old black Orthodox Jew who has tried to be an active
member of his Jewish community. "The experience that always
seems to bother me is that of being treated as an interloper or
transient no matter how long you remain in the community, or no
matter how involved you are," he complains. "The constant need
for others to validate your Jewishness because of your skin color.
The hesitancy of people to acknowledge you on Shabbos or Yom
Tov with a greeting. Some will stare right past you deliberately.
The overt stares and lack of respect of others. The assumption that
because of your race you are not knowledgeable."

On one occasion, Roxanne, a young, single black woman
visited a new synagogue for an evening Shabbat service. "I
entered the sanctuary and took a seat. I noticed that all the other
congregants seated themselves in little pods at least four rows
away from me. I was all by myself. The others all had siddurim,
but I had none. After the service a tray was passed around with
kiddush cups of wine. The server purposely passed me up and
did not even look at me nor offer me any wine. I ate a few cookies
while the congregants gathered in a cluster about 30 feet from me.

They sent over a spokesman to ask me if I was converting to Judaism. I responded, 'Yes.' He said, 'That's what we thought.' And he turned and went back to the cluster of congregants to report what I had said. I never returned to that shul."

Roxanne's experience was magnified by her obvious physical differences from the other congregants, but feelings of alienation, disconnection, and disaffiliation from the organized Jewish community are not limited to racially and ethnically diverse Jews. Jews of all kinds also feel that synagogues are not warm and welcoming enough, that Jewish institutions throw up socioeconomic obstacles at every turn, and that barriers to full participation seem too large to overcome.

People of all colors also have good experiences. In many cases, those who find the mainstream Jewish community welcoming are families rather than individuals. For years, Dorothy, a black Jew-by-choice, experienced rejection in Reform synagogues on the East Coast. Then she and her family moved to Portland, Oregon, where they joined a Reconstructionist synagogue and entered a new world. Perhaps typical of the West Coast, which tends to have a more transient population that is used to welcoming newcomers, Dorothy found the new congregation "accepting of differences and diversity. My synagogue is filled with wonderful people," she says, "who introduce themselves to be friendly, not nosy. In seventeen years [of participating in the Jewish community on the East Coast], I went to another person's house for Shabbat dinner only once (and they were next-door neighbors, not congregants). [My children] and I have been in Oregon for four months, and

> *The Jewish community benefits when racially and ethnically diverse Jews affiliate with multiracial/multicultural organizations, because their participation increases the visibility of diverse Jews in non-white communities.*

have already been to six Shabbat dinners and two parties. We have attended every *simcha* that's happening. We have never felt so warm and accepted."

As more people of color join Jewish organizations, the broader Jewish community is changed. Jews who know little or nothing of the existence of diverse Jews will become more aware of the person seated in the next chair. These organizations, as well as other Jewish groups, must not only make room for but actively seek a diverse membership. For their own future viability, these groups must work to ensure that they reflect the changing American Jewish population, which in turn will help to build a stronger Jewish community.

> Diverse Jews can be the most important players in the reduction of prejudice on any side of complex racial and religious equations. Their multiple identities give them multiple points of entry to teach, and by their very lives, to challenge and debunk stereotypes.

Community-building is not a purely internal task. While diverse Jews navigate their relationship to mainstream Jews, they are also managing their place within their respective ethnic and racial communities. Many communities of color assume that all Jews are white. The best way to counteract these stereotypes about Jews, including anti-Semitic attitudes, is from within. The result of more fruitful interaction between Jews and non-Jewish people of color could be a furthering of the Ahavas Sholom example, where people of color who are not Jews choose to participate in Jewish programs because they feel welcome and because they are "in the neighborhood."

The Jewish community benefits when racially and ethnically diverse Jews affiliate with multiracial/multicultural organizations, because their participation increases the visibility of diverse Jews in non-white communities. In the Institute for Jewish & Community Research study, nearly half the respondents (48%) were members of at least one such group. Not surprisingly, adoptive families, who are often headed by white parents with diverse children, were most likely to belong to these groups (59%), followed by Jewish families by conversion (43%) and Jewish families by birth/partnership (38%). In general, adoptive families are the best networked of all groups, since parents often seek support and information on a number of issues, including transracial families, adoption, and racial and cultural identity. The organizations that the study population joined included, among others, FCC (Families with Children from China), the NAACP, the Southern Poverty Law Center, TREC (Teach Respect for Every Culture), GIFT (Getting Interracial Families Together), LAPA (Latin American Parents Association), Amigos de Guatemala, Swirl (a non-profit social, support, and education organization for mixed-race people), Hapa Issues Forum (for mixed-race Asian Pacific Islander people), among others.

> *We cannot accept as immovable those boundaries that have long kept us apart, whether they are racial, ethnic, ideological, or other. The Jewish community, dedicated to the notion of one people and one God, simply cannot afford to turn against itself.*

Who better to build relationships between minority populations and the Jewish community than Jews of color? Diverse Jews can be great emissaries to the rest of the world. They are the bridge builders and the creators of dialogue. They can be the most important players in the reduction of prejudice on any side of complex racial and religious equations. Their multiple identities give them multiple points of entry to teach and, by their very lives, to challenge and debunk stereotypes.

Nonetheless, Jewish organizations need to find a way to bridge the gap within its own ranks, while it seeks to influence the larger racial discussion in the country. While any community-building effort must respect the needs of each subgroup within the larger Jewish community, we cannot accept as immovable those boundaries that have long kept us apart, whether they are racial, ethnic, ideological, or other. Healing the world—*tikkun olam*—must begin within our own home. The Jewish community, dedicated to the notion of one people and one God, simply cannot afford to turn against itself.

Toward a More Inclusive Future

Created by the Institute for Jewish & Community Research, *Be'chol Lashon (In Every Tongue)* is a research and community-building initiative to support a Jewish community that is more racially, ethnically, and culturally inclusive, both in the United States and around the world.

Be'chol Lashon avidly advocates for growth in the Jewish community, including proactive conversion, long the ultimate barrier to the growth of the Jewish people. The "who is a Jew" debate is passionate and can find people and institutions taking rigid positions. Proponents of either more inclusiveness, or of erecting the highest barriers against conversion, see their actions as the bulwark against the dissolution of the Jewish people. Institutional positioning revolves around ideologies that are heart-felt for those who care about the preservation and prosperity of the Jewish people. The battles are fierce because the stakes are so high.

Be'chol Lashon works to make Judaism accessible to non-Jewish partners of intermarried Jews, and to those seeking Judaism in communities in the United States, Africa, Asia, and South America. The Jewish community should encourage the millions of North Americans, Africans, South Americans, and Asians who identify with Judaism and the millions of Anusim who have not yet returned to Judaism to be part of the Jewish people. Such efforts could result in the Jewish population growing by millions over a ten-year period. "Opening the gates," as well as our hearts, means continuing efforts to include emerging Jewish communities around the world.

It is not enough to state that there should be programs within the Jewish community specifically for diverse Jews. The needs of diverse Jews are as varied as the backgrounds of the people themselves. Indeed, as this book has discussed, there is no singular group with a singular set of needs. In some circumstances, diverse Jews want to be with other Jews just like themselves: Latino Jews only with Latino Jews, African American Jews with African American Jews, and so on. Even within those smaller groupings, there may be a need for sub-groups, like transracially adopted Jews meeting other transracially adopted Jews. At different times, communities of color wish to join together. Diverse Jews, for example, may feel a sense of community simply from their status as "not of the mainstream." Finally, diverse Jews also want to participate in programs with the general Jewish population. The permutations of "community" are endless, and institutions that support diverse Jews must bear this in mind.

The existence of organizations, programs, and institutions, with their (sometimes) narrow constituencies and (often) suspicious attitudes towards others points to a paradox that the Jewish community should take into account when trying to provide for

> The Jewish community should encourage the millions of Americans, Africans, South Americans and Asians who identify with Judaism and the millions of Anusim who have not yet returned to Judaism to be part of the Jewish people.

the needs of extant diverse Jews and the potential of welcoming others. For any community to be strong, its minorities must feel respected and valued, while the overall community remains cohesive. For the American Jewish population, this translates to programming specifically for communities of color, as well as more inclusive programs for the larger Jewish population. The paradox is that targeted programming can create factionalism, dividing the community, but without it, minority members of the community may feel alienated and choose not to participate. The differences between the movements in Judaism, and their concomitant bickering over legitimacy, are one very obvious example in the Jewish community of driving people away. Race and ethnicity is another that requires vigilance.

It is not enough to state that there should be programs within the Jewish community specifically for diverse Jews. The needs of diverse Jews are as varied as the backgrounds of the people themselves.

Some efforts at programming for racially and ethnically diverse Jews exist both inside and outside the Jewish establishment. There are a smattering of programs at synagogues and Jewish community centers. A number of grassroots organizations have emerged to serve the population of ethnically and racially diverse Jews. There are programs for the transracial adoption community, camping weekends for racially and ethnically diverse Jews, support and study groups, newsletters, internet listservs, and so on.[1] Most are volunteer-run, with limited institutional structure, staff and financial resources.

So what needs to be done?

Be'chol Lashon has emerged as a systemic approach for promoting and embracing both growth and inclusion in the Jewish community. Be'chol Lashon is community-building writ large, deriving its agenda from the research of the Institute for Jewish & Community Research. Attitudinal and demographic information on the one hand and assessments of organizational cultures and capacity on the other hand provide the knowledge for action.

Be'chol Lashon acts as a central clearinghouse—partnering with business leaders, communal professionals, rabbis, and organizations to serve diverse Jews. Be'chol Lashon helps conceptualize and design programs—even envisioning new organizational structures—to address the needs uncovered in the Institute's research. The agenda is so vast, complicated, and challenging that more, rather than less, programmatic and organizational synergy is essential. Be'chol Lashon is the largest initiative of its kind in terms of people reached, communities involved, staff, and financial commitment. Be'chol Lashon supports the "best and brightest" in their leadership roles as community advisors, adjunct faculty, senior research associates, and research fellows. The current scope of the Be'chol Lashon initiative is explored in the following section.

> *Be'chol Lashon has emerged as a model for promoting and embracing both growth and inclusion in the Jewish community.*

Research

Qualitative and quantitative research drives the actions of Be'chol Lashon. Community-building is guided by information from all segments of the Jewish population. The research contained in this study is only the beginning. The Institute for Jewish & Community Research will continue to study communities of ethnically and racially diverse Jews. The Institute will also study the attitudes, beliefs, and behaviors of the larger Jewish community towards openness and inclusiveness as they relate not only to diverse Jews but also to Jews at the margins of mainstream, institutional Jewish life. They are the unaffiliated and the disaffected, those who cannot make it beyond the ideological and institutional barriers of the Jewish community. For diverse Jews, race and ethnicity play an obvious part in their sense of alienation from the Jewish community, but that cannot be the sole component. Too many white Jews also feel that the Jewish community is unwelcoming and rigid. The Institute is dedicated to producing information that will help the community to be more open and welcoming in order to grow.

The initial step that would later lead to the creation of Be'chol Lashon was the Institute's study to assess the landscape of ethnically and racially diverse Jews in the United States. Through inquiries to synagogues, Jewish community centers and other Jewish organizations, advertisements in newspapers and, most of all, through word of mouth, individuals stepped forward to tell their stories in interviews, focus groups and questionnaires. One young bi-racial Jewish woman's comment, "I have never seen another Jew who looks like me," captured the experience of many of the respondents in the focus groups. It was their demand for programming—the need to "see" others who looked like them— that inspired the next step: the birth of Be'chol Lashon as a research *and* community-building initiative.

Network Building

Be'chol Lashon creates networks among individuals and organizations through on-going conversations and individual meetings as well as workshops and conferences.

Be'chol Lashon Think Tank

Starting with a seminal international conference in 2002, Be'chol Lashon has sponsored an annual think tank for racially and ethnically diverse Jewish community leaders. Participants include current and emerging leaders from around the world, representing Jewish communities in Argentina, Brazil, Burundi, China, Ethiopia, India, Mexico, Nigeria, Portugal, South Africa, Spain, Uganda, and Zimbabwe, among others. From within the United States, rabbis of all colors and branches of Judaism, secular Jews, mixed-race Jews, and a broad range of scholars, activists, professionals, and community organizers are part of this gathering, including representatives of many "mainstream" organizations. At these conferences, people who might otherwise remain in their own isolated enclaves meet to develop networks, friendships, and partnerships, to learn from each other and to exchange information. Topics for workshops and panel discussions have included: navigating multiple identities, building bridges among communities of Jews, the role of the synagogue in community-building, coalition-building among organizations, promoting outreach and growth, and combating resurgent anti-Semitism.

Gathering such a group of diverse people gives participants a view of how varied the Jewish community really is and therefore helps to promote tolerance and, ultimately, unity. People who would not normally find themselves seated at the same table (African American Orthodox men, for example, beside Asian American Reform lesbians) find that they have a respectful forum in which to explore their deepest feelings, hopes, and fears about themselves and the "other" within the Jewish community. As one African American woman said in a workshop on building bridges, "The key is education. People need to know that we exist. I have to go on record that when I heard that there were gay and lesbian Jews, [I was upset] because my upbringing told me that it was wrong. But, the Torah is not here for us to judge. [...] Now I will allow room in my heart for gays to worship like everyone else, and they will be with Hashem."[2]

A number of initiatives for systemic institutional and communal change have emerged from the annual think tanks.

After meeting for three years, African and African American Jewish leaders formed the Pan African Jewish Alliance (PAJA). The Pan African Jewish Alliance is devoted to furthering the development and growth of Jewish communities throughout Africa. PAJA also seeks to integrate African and African-American Jews into the mainstream Jewish community.

At this same meeting, the World Federation of Anusim Communities was formed by Latino/Hispanic Jewish leaders devoted to helping bring back to Judaism those of Spanish and Portuguese descent. The goal of the Federation of Anusim Communities is to coordinate efforts to welcome and facilitate the return of Anusim (descendants of Jews forced to convert to Catholicism during the Inquisition) to Judaism, including assisting them in halakhic return/conversion.

Both emerging coalitions represent the possibility of a more inclusive future for diverse Jews around the world and could result in millions of additional African and Latino Jews.

Ongoing Conversations, Meetings and Workshops

The annual conference is supplemented with dialogue throughout the year, to build trust and deepen the relationships that begin in the larger setting. Ongoing meetings and workshops now take place throughout the year among the individuals and communities represented at the conference in various locations across the country—Los Angles, Chicago, New York and Philadelphia. The results of building trust can be surprising, leading to fruitful contact with individuals and communities that might otherwise remain invisible to each other, as well as to the majority white community. For example, the Israelite Board of Rabbis represents some black Jewish communities primarily in New York, Chicago, and Philadelphia, but they also have ties to groups in Virginia, Barbados, and elsewhere. Israelite rabbis and their congregants often have had a history of negative experiences from their limited contact with the majority Jewish community. After a number of conversations, it became clear that some African American congregations would like to connect to the majority of Jews, but they previously had had no points of entry.

National and International Conferences

Be'chol Lashon sponsors diverse Jewish leaders to attend other national and international conferences. In 2004, Rabbi Capers Funnye and Professor Ephraim Isaac were Be'chol Lashon representatives at the Conference of World Religions in Barcelona, Spain, and Professor Isaac, an Ethiopian/Yemenite Jew, was the keynote speaker at an historic meeting of the Society of Ethiopian Jewish Studies in Addis Ababa, Ethiopia. It is important that the larger society sees the multi-ethnic/racial character of the Jewish community.

Be'chol Lashon Newsletter

In addition to the ongoing meetings throughout the year, it is important for Jewish communities around the world to stay abreast of issues that affect diverse Jews. The Institute for Jewish & Community Research distributes a bi-monthly Be'chol Lashon Newsletter via email as well as posting it on the Institute's website.[3] The newsletter contains items of interest from worldwide Jewish communities. It serves to further educate isolated Jewish communities about the policies and practices of other Jewish communities, and to educate Jews in the mainstream about diverse Jews with whom they may not be familiar.

Community Support
Technical Assistance

Be'chol Lashon works with diverse Jewish leaders to help define and achieve their community goals. Be'chol Lashon conceptualizes and facilitates workshops that are tailored to address individual communal needs. For example, a number of African American synagogues requested technical assistance on how to most effectively manage their congregations. In 2004, Be'chol Lashon, in partnership with Professor Lewis Gordon and the Center for Afro-Jewish Studies at Temple University, sponsored a financial management workshop in Philadelphia attended by forty rabbis, treasurers, and board members of African American synagogues from New York, Chicago and Philadelphia. Topics included board development and building relationships with financial institutions. The workshop featured a panel of representatives from banks in New York, Chicago, and Philadelphia that specialize in faith-based lending.

Building Local Community

Communities are built by people; relationships are not institutional, but personal. To that end, it is essential that local communities create and promulgate programs for diverse Jews so that, if nothing else, people can literally set eyes upon each other.

> *Communities are built by people; relationships are not institutional, but personal.*

Breaking the curse of invisibility is the first step towards understanding. In the Institute for Jewish & Community Research study, an overwhelming 93% of respondents felt that it was either "very important" (68%) or "somewhat important" (25%) to have more programs in the Jewish community that included racially and ethnically diverse Jews. (See Figure 7.) As Joanie, a 29-year-old mixed-race woman, said, "I would like to see Jewish institutions create space for Jews of color to congregate and meet each other." Hopefully over time, mainstream synagogues will become more diverse (90% see the need). Respondents also felt that both Jewish holiday celebrations (87%) and social/recreational networks (86%)

offered important opportunities for all kinds of Jews to meet and get to know each other.

In the San Francisco Bay Area, for example, the Bay Area Be'chol Lashon sponsors and organizes holiday events such as Chanukah celebrations and Shavuot festivals for racially and ethnically diverse Jews. In 2000, the first Chanukah celebration in the San Francisco Bay Area brought together two groups of Jews: African American converts, who exhibited a joyful sense of their Jewish identity, and Jews with one white Jewish parent and one black non-Jewish parent, who tended to experience conflict between their racial and religious identities. At subsequent holiday events, this original group of 60 has grown to over 400, and has expanded to include black, Asian, Latino and mixed-race Jews by birth, choice, and adoption, as well as their families and friends.

Some Bay Area Be'chol Lashon events are "by invitation only" to diverse Jews and their families and friends as part of a targeted outreach strategy, which has helped create a strong sense of community. Other Be'chol Lashon programs cast a wide net and

Figure 7

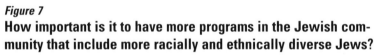

How important is it to have more programs in the Jewish community that include more racially and ethnically diverse Jews?

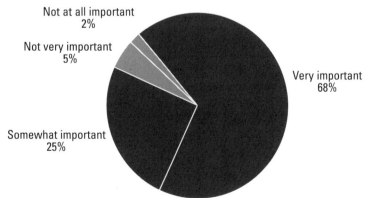

Source: *Survey of Racially & Ethnically Diverse Jews in the United States, Institute for Jewish & Community Research, 2001.*

are geared toward educating the general public. These events garner a variety of mainstream organizational support, with the Shavuot Festival, for example, attracting 40 co-sponsoring organizations in 2004, and 50 in 2005, including federations, synagogues, day schools, Jewish community centers, and others.

Individuals who participated in the Institute for Jewish & Community Research study, as well as attendees at the Bay Area Be'chol Lashon events, routinely ask for additional programming, including Jewish learning programs (76% of survey respondents), retreats for diverse Jews (70%), youth groups (67%), and *havurot* (66%). (See Figure 8.) By popular demand, programming in the Bay Area has expanded to include an annual weekend retreat. There are also requests for specialized support for those anticipating life cycle events such as b'nei mitzvot, marriage, and birth.

As a case study with five years of successful experience, Bay Area Be'chol Lashon has developed a replicable model for local programming that is expanding to the New York, Chicago and Los Angeles communities. Leaders from each of these geographic areas have been integral in planning and executing programming in the San Francisco Bay Area over the years: Rabbi Funnye in Chicago, Rabbi Manny Viñas in New York, and Davi Cheng and Miri Hunter Haruach, Ph.D., in Los Angeles. The continuity in leadership will ensure a smooth transition from place to place, tailoring the best practices of the Bay Area programming to suit the character of individual communities.

Recruitment

One of the greatest challenges in creating local programming for diverse Jews is that many in the target population may not be affiliated with an institution. Or even more challenging, they may have no contact whatsoever with the Jewish community or be suspicious because of negative experiences in the past. It is imperative, then, that groups seeking to develop local events create effective methods to identify, locate, and attract diverse Jews. Be'chol Lashon devotes significant effort to recruitment. According to the Jewish Outreach Institute's 2005 Bay Area community scan:

> Be'chol Lashon's follow-up is personalized, with program operators able to track newcomers and participants' engagement in programming, thereby facilitating relationship building. When re-connecting with past participants in order to invite them to the next event, they not only send a mailing but also work the phones to a degree unmatched by any other organization. Thanks to a detailed and well-organized database, they're able to access each participant's information while making calls, allowing them to reference personal information (such as

Figure 8
Interest in programs for racially/ethnically diverse Jews
(Percent interested)

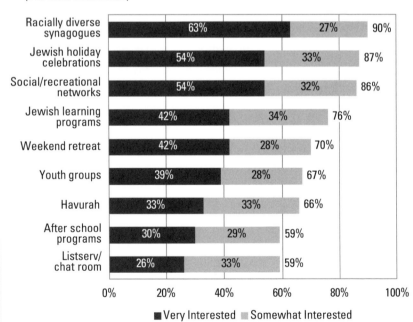

Source: *Survey of Racially & Ethnically Diverse Jews in the United States, Institute for Jewish & Community Research, 2001.*

children's names) that greatly strengthens the relationship. In addition, Be'chol Lashon is a prime example of an organization that serves as a gateway into deeper engagement for newcomers.[4]

Scholarships

Many Jewish institutions have traditionally constructed barriers that are foreboding to many potential members and participants, including high fee structures and distrustful attitudes (although nearly all would define themselves as warm, open, and welcoming). It is important to remove disincentives that may contribute to keeping people away from Jewish institutions and programs. One step in welcoming more people is to bridge the financial gap that keeps many people away. For example, Bay Area Be'chol Lashon holiday events are free, which effectively eliminates one of the greatest barriers to participation: cost. For other programs like the retreat, the Be'chol Lashon inclusion policy is clear: if someone is considering not participating for financial reasons, that individual or family is eligible to receive scholarship aid. No questions asked. Unaffiliated and disenfranchised individuals have no tolerance to be scrutinized in the typical scholarship application process, however well intentioned.

Scholarships for children to attend synagogues, Jewish day schools, and summer camps increase the racial/ethnic diversity of those institutions and programs. This is not meant to imply that families with children of color cannot afford to send their children to Jewish day schools and summer camps. Rather, it is a recognition that the financial barrier that keeps out Jews of all types may be felt particularly by those who already question whether they will find a welcoming place inside the gates. Additionally, some parents of racially and ethnically diverse children do not want their child to be the only person like himself or herself at a particular Jewish institution. Scholarships provide an incentive for parents to send their children to predominantly white institutions, and an increase in attendance of children of color can have a snowball effect, attracting even more diverse Jews.

Education
Break the Cycle of Ignorance

During a workshop entitled, "Building Bridges among Communities of Jews" at the 2004 Be'chol Lashon Think Tank in San Francisco, Rachel, a white Reconstructionist rabbi, was asked how the Jewish Renewal movement approached the topic of racially and ethnically diverse Jews. She replied, "They don't know about you! It was news to me. I went to [an Orthodox gathering] and met a black Jew once. I was surprised. I had never met an American black Jew before her. It is education. No Jew would watch you in a service and say that you are not a Jew. We, the white Jews, can learn from you. The sacredness expressed. People have to see you, no argument about it. People need to become friends. That will build the bridges."[5] Communal education is an essential way to break the cycle of ignorance that keeps mainstream Jews like Rachel from recognizing the existence of diverse Jews. Education should be a many-pronged effort.

Visual Representations - Speaker's Bureau & Film

It is essential that visual representations of Jews of color be created and disseminated. To reach into mainstream Jewish communities, into non-Jewish minority communities, and into the general population, Be'chol Lashon has developed a speaker's bureau of diverse Jews. Many Jews of color want to speak out in support of Israel and against anti-Semitism. As members of racial minorities, diverse Jews are likely to be better received and have greater impact when speaking about prejudice and racism than mainstream Jews in America. The growth of anti-Semitism and anti-Israelism on college campuses is a specific area of concern. As noted earlier, much of the debate takes place within the paradigm of race: Jews are the "white oppressors" of Palestinians, who are portrayed as persecuted people of color. Having diverse Jews speak about their own experiences helps to frame the discussion in a different light.

Be'chol Lashon is also co-producing a documentary film entitled, *Judaism and Race in America*, co-directed by Avishai Yeganyahu Mekonen and Shari Rothfarb Mekonen. Mr. Mekonen is an Ethiopian-Israeli filmmaker who recently immigrated to the United States, and Ms. Rothfarb Mekonen is an American film-maker and professor at Borough of Manhattan Community College / City University of New York. Shortly after arriving in the United States, Avishai soon realized that Americans in general, and many in the majority Jewish community in particular, did not recognize him as a Jew. He became increasingly aware that the Jews of color in this country were often isolated, largely ignorant about each other, and inadequately inte-

As members of racial minorities, diverse Jews are likely to be better received and have greater impact when speaking about prejudice and racism than mainstream Jews in America.

grated into the Jewish community at large. The film explores how Jewish identity is constructed within the context of race. The distribution venues include film festivals, public television, and Jewish and non-Jewish educational organizations.

Curriculum Development

A fundamental part of education is curriculum development: textbooks, lesson plans, and multi-media classroom material. In most Jewish curricula, the diversity of the Jewish people, if it is depicted at all, is often poorly represented. In most educational settings, neither the content nor the visual representations in the teaching materials adequately reflect the complexity and variety of contemporary Jewish communities around the world. Nor do representations of Biblical scenes that took place in Africa accurately reflect the people of that region. Jewish children will be better informed Jews and better informed Americans if they learn about the richness of Jewish communities in Africa, South America, and Asia. In addition, a more accurate portrayal of Jews and Jewish history will help to defray misperceptions by the general population that perpetuate negative stereotypes of Jews and Israel.

Rabbinic and Professional Development
Professional Development

For the Jewish community to thrive, its leaders must reflect the people they lead. Rabbis and other professionals who serve diverse Jews require specific skills, knowledge, and sensitivity to the complex issues that affect those communities. The Jewish community must build the capacity to develop more rabbis to serve the growing diverse population, and in particular, to assist racially and ethnically diverse Jews who are interested in becoming rabbis. Financial support in the form of fellowships for Africans, Asians, Latinos, and African Americans who wish to train to be rabbis, scholars, and teachers is a cornerstone of strengthening the community.

Fellowships

Be'chol Lashon initiated a fellowship program to assist individuals as they become more effective community leaders. For example, it was the dream of Rabbi Gershom Sizomu, the spiritual leader of the Abayudaya Jews of Uganda, to attend rabbinic school in the United States. The Institute is sponsoring

Rabbi Sizomu and his family to live in the United States (and Israel) to attend rabbinic school for five years where is he is currently a rabbinic student at the Ziegler School of Rabbinic Studies at the University of Judaism with the help of partners in the Los Angeles community, including the University of Judaism, Kadima Day School, Congregation Shomrei Torah, and a number of dedicated individuals. In his capacity as a fellow at the Institute, he is educating Jews in the United States about Jews in Uganda, with the goal of strengthening his community in Uganda and Jewish communities throughout Africa. After completing his rabbinic training, he will return to Uganda to lead his community. At that point, he will be well positioned to fulfill his dream of opening a pan-African yeshiva to provide the rabbinic training that other Africans are requesting but is not available. Through his Be'chol Lashon fellowship, Rabbi Sizomu will achieve his goal of earning a rabbinic degree as well as laying the groundwork for bringing economic opportunity to his community, including utilities, medical facilities, more education, and cottage industries.

Rabson Wuriga is an emerging leader of the Lemba in South Africa, Zimbabwe, and Mozambique. He earned his Ph.D. in philosophy from the University of Natal in Durban, South Africa, in anticipation of assuming a leadership role in the Lemba community. As a research fellow of Be'chol Lashon and the Center for Afro-Jewish Studies, Temple University, he is working with the Lemba Cultural Association and others to research and document the traditions of the Lemba. His goal is to help the 100,000 or more dispersed Lemba, many of whom are eager to return to Jewish ritual practice, and broaden and deepen their participation in Jewish life.

Challenges

The Be'chol Lashon initiative faces difficult challenges. It functions at the nexus of some of the most problematic aspects of our society—racial politics, strong religious and ideological differences, and institutional turf battles. Community-building involves both individuals and groups, all of whom bring their personalities and their collective group memories with them. Progress is hard, and often slow. Because racial and religious politics include the narratives of accumulated wrongs and grievances, it should not be surprising to encounter unresolved issues from the past. Many Jews carry with them the accumulated memory of being a persecuted minority, and racially and ethnically diverse often carry a dual narrative of discrimination. Community-building not only involves addressing conflicts, but sometimes working around them. Creating a positive Judaism means ameliorating the narrative of victimhood. Healing will take some time.

But there is also reason for optimism. Be'chol Lashon is at the beginning of a long journey. Achievements will be measured in small steps forward—a program here, a relationship there. Institutional relationships are being forged. People who are historically suspicious about one another are sitting around tables at workshops and conferences and also worshipping together. The politics of race and religion, as contentious as they are, do not prohibit progress.

Who Is a Jew, Really?

Jewish theology, ritual observance, social customs and language have all evolved over the millennia in a variety of ways. There has never been, nor likely will there be any single authentic Judaism. Jews have no Pope, catechism, or theological tribunal. Liturgy, ritual observance, and social interaction all change and evolve, and there has been tremendous latitude and variety among Jewish cultures over time and place, with ongoing reinterpretation and adjustment. New ideas and practices invariably populate the Jewish landscape. Beliefs and activities come and go, institutions are created and abandoned, great bodies of knowledge consistently added to and reconfigured. Various levels of Orthodox, Conservative, Reform, Reconstructionist, and other movements add to the richness of the landscape of Jewish life. Each has something to say and something legitimate to offer. It is time to recognize the next evolution.

The issues that arise in thinking about racially and ethnically diverse Jews point to the most important questions facing the Jewish community today: What is the basis for our identity as Jews? Are we open to converts? How do we deal with intermarriage? Who are we talking about when we talk about "the Jewish people"?

These uncertain boundaries raise difficult questions. If there are no central authorities or universally accepted criteria to determine who is a Jew, is there any practice, trait, or custom that we can identify as unquestionably Jewish? Or, are we faced with such a broad spectrum that Judaism has no boundaries, that one can be Jewish simply by declaring oneself a Jew? All groups have points of entry, rules for admission, and procedures to be included. How these rules are defined and administered and who makes them is another set of issues. We can find the answers only if we are willing to challenge our biases and rethink our assumptions.

> *All groups have points of entry, rules for admission, and procedures to be included. How these rules are defined and administered, and who makes them is another set of issues.*

As this book shows, few topics in Jewish life are as interesting and complicated as its diversity. We have forgotten that Jews have survived for so many years by adapting to and adopting from the communities in which we have lived. Having lived practically everywhere on the planet over thousands of years, we have become diverse by language, custom, ideology, spiritual practice, ethnicity, and skin tone. Becoming like the people who surround us is not the end of the Jewish people but rather another step in our evolution. We are already white, black, Asian, Latino, mixed-race. We are already a global community. How extraordinary and exciting to be part of a people that is composed of relatives from practically every branch of the human family.

As Americans, we embrace diversity. After all, the American people (like the Jewish people) are an amalgam of the world. American Jews are then truly "twice blessed," the most diverse people in the most diverse nation. Our multi-faceted character in this open and welcoming society is the key to Jewish survival and prosperity, but only if we move towards our manifold identity instead of running away from it. Ironically, in a country where the metaphors for the blending of peoples range from melting pots to tossed salads, some Jews have persistently chosen to ignore or combat our own many flavors. That much feared goblin, assimilation, and its henchman, intermarriage, have become such villains in contemporary Jewish mythology that we have purposefully kept out of our consciousness all reminders that we have never in our history been homogeneous. We represent so many peoples on earth, because we have lived among them, adopted their cultures, married their sons and daughters, and over time assumed their physical characteristics. Jewish survival is often credited to tradition, those ineluctable practices that transcend time and place. Jewish survival owes just as much to our adaptability across time, whether by choice or by necessity.[1]

> *Becoming like the people who surround us is not the end of the Jewish people but rather another step in our evolution. We are already white, black, Asian, Latino, mixed-race. We are already a global people.*

We are a complex bunch. We are petrified of disappearing but are equally afraid of losing our status as a beleaguered group. We do not like being marginalized, but we like being just special enough to maintain our outsider/insider status. We crave to be part of the American mainstream but not swept away in it. It is no wonder that the relationship between majority and diverse Jews is so complicated. Diverse Jews represent all the pushes and pulls of our complicated Jewish psyche.

This book is as much about growth as it is about diversity, the cornerstone of a healthy community. We need to grow in numbers, in spiritual depth, in our community infrastructure, in our knowledge, and in our ability to make the world a better place. As the Jewish community grows, it will continue to become more diverse. That diversity is our strength and our future. We cannot grow and prosper without becoming more open and welcoming. An ideological and structural makeover of the Jewish community is necessary if we are to remain a healthy and thriving community.

At this point, a miniscule financial commitment comes from the Jewish community for these purposes. To move into our future, the Jewish community must invest in the actual vision, design, and implementation needed to remake itself. What the community needs is a new institutional framework in which visionary leaders can work to help direct and mold the future of Jewish life. Some of this investment is already taking place in grassroots organizations, programs, and projects springing up all over the United States. Programs within existing institutions and outside them show incredible promise for redefining the Jewish future. Breaking the constraints of the current system—investing in the new, the different, the strange and the exciting—remolds the Jewish community.

> *Jewish survival is often credited to tradition. Jewish survival owes just as much to our adaptability across time, whether by choice or by necessity.*

We must modify our core attitudes, beliefs, and actions. If intermarriage is deemed a threat to the long-term survival of the Jewish people, then the community must make every effort to welcome the non-Jewish partners of Jews and provide a supportive, affirming place for their children to develop a Jewish identity. If more and more Jews are adopting transracially, then the community must expand its definition of what makes a family. And, if Judaism, despite its acquired suspicion of outsiders and its archaic practices of turning away those who ask to join, remains attractive to those persistent individuals of color who still find solace, inspiration, and joy in the Jewish community, then the community must change its definition of what a Jew looks like. In the face of the changing demographics of the American population, we must move beyond our current state of self-imposed ignorance or risk nourishing the roots of our own irrelevance.

This work is dedicated to a more vibrant and alive Jewish community. American and world Jewry are both entering the next phase. The doom-and-gloomers who predict the demise of the Jewish community, its continued shrinking and loss of identity, would be well advised to read the findings of this research. There are hundreds of thousands—perhaps millions of Americans and others around the globe—of all races and ethnicities who could be Jewish. Are we ready to welcome them? Are we ready to grow and change? Are we willing to become who we have always been?

Be'chol Lashon: A Visual Journey

San Francisco Bay Area Be'chol Lashon sponsors an annual Chanukah party. Rabbi Capers Funnye (center), a spiritual leader of the Be'chol Lashon community, leads the children in the lighting of Chanukah candles.

Hundreds of celebrants from a multitude of races and ethnicities attend the annual Chanukah party. The programming includes all-family gatherings as well as activities designed for specific age groups.

Be'chol Lashon events build positive Jewish identities through informal education such as Jewish-related crafts projects. Adult counselors guide the children in the creation of hanukiyot *(Chanukah menorahs).*

The children carry home their experiences of celebrating holidays with other diverse Jews through their crafts projects.

Children feel the joy of Jewish holidays through activities like painting their own dreidels (four-sided tops) with Hebrew letters and learning to play the dreidel game.

Projects are inspired by the diversity of the Jewish people. Handmade spice boxes, filled with African, West Indian, and European spices, are used during the beautiful Havdalah ceremony on Saturday evening, reminding Jews of the sweetness of Shabbat.

At the Chanukah party, lighthearted physical activities, like tying and untying a human knot, teach celebrants how the Jewish people found themselves in a "bind" at different points in their history.

Even the youngest of those who attend Be'chol Lashon events have only to glance around them to see that any face can be a Jewish face.

Chanukah commemorates the rededication of the Jewish Temple in Jerusalem. Elementary school–age children "rededicate" the Temple by writing their hopes and wishes on paper bricks.

Programming captivates and educates children, from toddlers to teens. The holiday events provide time for small groups to learn together and to get to know each other.

Drumming, a centerpiece of Be'chol Lashon holiday celebrations, creates instant bonds among people of different ages and backgrounds.

Children learn holiday songs from different cultures and sing in Hebrew, English, Spanish, and other languages.

San Francisco Bay Area Be'chol Lashon, along with over 50 co-sponsors, hosts a Shavuot Festival that is free and open to the public. Shavuot celebrates the giving of the Torah to the Jewish people.

Food at Be'chol Lashon events reflects the multicultural participants. At the Shavuot Festival in 2004, celebrants enjoyed Senegalese cuisine.

Be'chol Lashon is both professionally organized and community-based. Dr. Denise Davis, a member of the Bay Area Be'chol Lashon Advisory Board, holds her daughter, Aviva, while she asks the Be'chol Lashon community for support for further programming.

The members of the public who attend the Shavuot Festival see, often for the first time, many different types of Jews celebrating their Judaism.

Inviting the public to a holiday celebration for diverse Jews also means building coalitions among many racial, ethnic, and religious communities. Members of the Jewish and African American Youth Alliance (JAAYA) perform at the Shavuot Festival.

Jewish religious rituals are part of Be'chol Lashon events. Rabbi Funnye, accompanied by helpers, teaches the Shehekiyanu *in Hebrew and in English, a prayer commemorating new beginnings.*

People who attend Be'chol Lashon holiday celebrations can choose those activities that most appeal to them, from religious observances and community-building workshops, to pure fun like face painting.

Shavuot is also a celebration of the inclusiveness of Judaism. It is a recognition that Jewish families have many faces!

At the Shavuot Festival, children create cheerful flowers from paper. Decorative paper cut-outs to celebrate spring are a tradition in both Mexican culture (called papel picado *in Spanish) and in Ashkenazi Jewish culture (called* shavuoslech *in Yiddish).*

A child mimicking a juggler entertains the crowd. Children who experience joy in Jewish activities grow up with strong and positive Jewish identities.

Every Be'chol Lashon celebration includes a multicultural book fair with offerings on topics as varied as identity, adoption, child-raising, folklore, and Jewish spirituality.

American Jews learn about global communities of Jews through the sale of items like kippot *(skull caps),* tallit *(prayer shawls),* challah *(ceremonial bread) covers, and music from Uganda, Ghana, Nigeria, and Israel. All proceeds go to back to the communities.*

Bay Area Be'chol Lashon has grown strong through large holiday celebrations and smaller, more intensive community-building events like the annual retreat.

Friendships formed during the weekend gathering last throughout the year. Children at the retreat are divided into age-specific groups, giving their parents an opportunity to attend workshops and other adult activities.

Community building fosters friendships among the children. The hula hoop challenge course teaches the five-to-eight-year-olds about cooperation.

For the children of Be'chol Lashon, consistent exposure to diverse Jews helps them feel secure in their Jewish identities.

Holding the retreat at a rural educational conference center gives the children the opportunity to explore their relationship with nature as well as with each other.

Outdoor activities keep the rapt attention of even the most easily distracted group of nine-to-twelve-year-olds, as they prepare to canoe on the lake.

Children have the opportunity to attend classes throughout the retreat. This group learns that sharing personal stories reinforces their diverse Jewish identities.

The children, guided by counselors, learn about the power of a drumming circle as a way of building community.

One young participant designs ...   models ...

and proudly wears her mask to celebrate her place in the community of diverse Jews.

The last evening of the annual retreat gathers together all age groups and their parents to see a play conceived, written, designed, choreographed, composed, and performed by the children, including the sometimes challenging teenagers.

After the play, participants at the annual retreat dance and celebrate the expanding and deepening of the Bay Area Be'chol Lashon community.

The diverse Jewish community leaders who participate in the annual Be'chol Lashon International Think Tank are at the forefront of their fields. They, and others like them, are working to create a more inclusive Jewish community.

Lewis Gordon, Ph.D., The Laura N. Carnell Chair of Philosophy at Temple University, is the founder of the Center for Afro-Jewish Studies and one of the foremost race theorists in the world.

Ephraim Isaac, Ph.D., is the director of the Institute of Semitic Studies. His linguistic skill, knowledge, and experience allows him an expansive sphere of influence among religious groups throughout the world.

Rabson Wuriga, Ph.D., a philosopher and biblical scholar by training, is a research fellow of the Institute for Jewish & Community Research. He was born in Zimbabwe and belongs to the Hamisi (or Hamish) clan of the Lemba Jewish community of Southern Africa.

Rabbi Capers Funnye, is the charis-matic Israelite spiritual leader of Beth Shalom in Chicago, where his wife Mary is active in the sisterhood. Rabbi Funnye is a member of the Chicago Board of Rabbis, and senior research associate of the Institute for Jewish & Community Research.

Dele Jane Osawe is an Ibo Jew and the first woman to be elected to political office from her senatorial district in Nigeria. She is a passionate advocate for both Ibo and Pan-African commu-nity development.

Rabbi Capers Funnye (far right) leads the congregants of Beth Shalom B'nai Zaken Ethiopian Hebrew Congregation in Chicago, to Tashlich *(symbolically casting away sins) on* Rosh Hashanah, *the Jewish New Year.*

Carlos Salas Díaz, who converted while studying at the University of Judaism, is the spiritual leader of Congregación Hebrea in Tijuana, Mexico. Like the majority of his congregants, he is the descendant of Conversos.

Aharon Franco lives in Cartagena, Murcia, Spain. He is the president of Agudat Sefarad and is an advocate for the recovery of the Sephardic legacy and the return of B'nei Anusim (descendants of Spanish and Portuguese Jews) to Judaism.

Rabbi Rigoberto Emmanuel Viñas, spiritual leader of Lincoln Park Jewish Center, New York, is the founder of El Centro de Estudios Judíos-Torat Emet, a Spanish-language house of study (bet midrash) whose mission is to serve as a resource for Conversos (Anusim) who wish to return to Judaism.

Rabbi Gershom Sizomu, the spiritu-
al leader of the Abayudaya Jews of
Uganda, attends the Ziegler School
of Rabbinic Studies, University of
Judaism, Los Angles as fellow of the
Institute for Jewish & Community
Research.

J.J. Keki is Gershom Sizomu's brother.
He is a successful farmer and local
political leader, the first Abayudaya to
be elected to government office in a
region with a majority of Christians
and Muslims.

*The Abayudaya Jews of Uganda are an example of a vibrant Jewish community
that has maintained their religious practice for three generations, often in the
face of hostility. Today, they live openly as Jews and work in cooperation with
their Christian and Muslim neighbors.*

Romiel Daniel was president of the
Magen Abraham Synagogue in
Ahmedabad, India and is currently
president of the Rego Park Jewish
Center and "The Jews of India" organi-
zation, New York. He conducts High
Holiday services in the Bene Israel
tradition.

Michael Menashe was born in
Manipur state in Northeast India.
He made aliyah to Israel and advo-
cates on behalf of the B'nei Menashe
community in both Israel and in
India.

Robin Washington, editorial page
editor of the Duluth News-Tribune,
discusses how Jews of color are portrayed in the media.

Michelle Stein-Evers Frankl teaches
about diverse Jews at the Melton
Graduate Program of the Shalom
Institute, University of New South
Wales, Australia.

Born in Hong Kong, Davi Cheng is the president of Beth Chayim Chadashim ("House of New Life") in Los Angeles, the world's first gay and lesbian synagogue, founded in 1972. Davi designed and helped fabricate the stained glass windows at the synagogue.

Carolivia Herron, Ph.D., a creative writer and advocate for diversity education in the United States, reads her groundbreaking children's book, "Nappy Hair."

Miri Hunter Haruach, Ph.D., the founder/director of Project Sheba in Los Angeles, is a women's spirituality workshop leader and performing artist.

Methodology

The data sources for this study were varied and extensive. Both quantitative and qualitative methods were utilized including:

- Mailed questionnaire
- Personal interviews
- Telephone interviews
- Internet interviews and email exchange
- Focus groups
- Program evaluations
- Site visits

These multiple approaches allowed a comprehensive and in-depth analysis of individual attitudes as well as of community values and procedures.

The Institute for Jewish & Community Research's estimate of the diverse Jewish population comes from our survey of the Jewish population conducted in 2002. The estimates of Jews of color are subject to large sampling error, since the sample size of Jewish households is so small compared to the overall population of the United States. The margin of error on this estimate is such that we treat these estimates of diverse Jews as indicators and not as a firm numbers. As with all estimates of Jews, the count also will vary as a function of definitions of who is a Jew.

Over 100 personal interviews were conducted between 2000 and 2004. The interviews included samples of adoptive parents, converts, mixed-race Jews, religiously mixed families, and multi-generational families of diverse Jews. Most of the interviews were conducted with individuals from the United States, plus a number with representatives from Africa, South America, and Asia. Some of those interviewed were selected because they were organizational leaders or scholars. Most interviewees were selected as representatives of a particular sub-population, e.g., mixed-race Jews.

An almost equal number of telephone interviews were conducted, including a few follow-ups from the personal interviews. By conducting up to five or more interviews with some individuals, we were able to explore in great depth the complexity and nuances of certain issues, such as interactions within families. Some telephone interviews were also necessary because time and cost factors did not permit personal interviews in every city in the country.

The Institute facilitated a series of focus group interviews in November 2000, which were repeated over the next five years. We conducted group interviews for biracial Jews, others for black Jews (the majority of whom were converts to Judaism), and a third group for Latino Jews. The group interviews provided these populations with the rare opportunity to be in the presence of other people like themselves. The group discussions each lasted about two hours.

The focus group interviewers gathered basic demographic information such as age, place of birth, and marital status. The facilitators then progressed to questions about family background and participants' feelings about Judaism, race, and their own identities as Jews who were not white. Overall, people expressed genuine excitement about having the opportunity to be part of a group of Jews like themselves. It was a deeply emotional moment for participants in each group when the facilitators asked people whether they would want to get together again. Some were outwardly excited and some could not speak at all, overwhelmed at the possibility of forming a community of other Jews like themselves. All of the group participants expressed interest in having more events for diverse Jews like themselves. Many were eager to have an opportunity to be with one another in informal social settings. Parents were also excited at the prospect of having their children meet. Although the focus groups were a research tool, each group immediately began forming a community.

The Institute also conducted group discussions in small workshop formats from 2000 to 2005 at a number of events. These discussions replicated some of the focus groups and provided information about additional subpopulations like religiously mixed families, among others. At three Be'chol Lashon International Think Tanks, similar group discussions were held among leaders from diverse communities, including rabbis, scholars, and directors of organizations. Over thirty group discussions were held in all.

Email communications were an additional source of data, some in the form of structured questions, and some as informal conversation and dialogue. These emails produced stories about personal journeys and experiences with Jewish communal institutions. Sometimes the emails were almost stream-of-consciousness and served a therapeutic function. Together with the personal interviews and focus groups, the emails helped fill in the gaps on many of the critical issues of concern for diverse Jews and their families.

The Institute conducted a number of events and programs for diverse Jews in the Bay Area. Program evaluations proved to be a rich data source. Each program conducted by the Institute, including a lecture series featuring diverse Jews and holiday celebrations (Chanukah and Shavuot), utilized evaluation questionnaires. These included demographic background and questions about the kinds of programs and events that participants would like to have available in the community. Cumulatively, the program evaluations helped assess the programmatic needs for diverse Jews.

The research also involved site visits by the principal investigators to a number of diverse organizations. This included Beth Shalom B'nai Zaken Ethiopian Hebrew Congregation in Chicago, Temple Beth'El in Philadelphia, the Israelite Board of Rabbis, and B'nai Adath Kol Beth Yisrael in Brooklyn. These visits provided a much deeper understanding of the existing and emerging institutional structure serving diverse Jews.

The Institute also conducted a mail survey in 2001 completed by over 300 individuals. Our mailed questionnaire was sent to a non-random sample from a database of diverse Jews collected via the internet, newspaper advertisements for the study, word of mouth, and Be'chol Lashon program participants who volunteered their contact information both for future program announcements and to be part of the research. The Be'chol Lashon database continues to grow through these techniques. Some biases, which may be introduced through self-selection, cannot be measured.

The survey included questions about identity, community needs, and family structure. The 313 completed surveys in this study included data about 1,010 people: 527 adults and 483 children, either diverse Jews or people who are part of families that included at least one diverse Jew. The response rate was 31%, excellent for a mailed questionnaire. Thirty-six states were represented in the study. States that had no representatives were primarily those with small Jewish populations such as North and South Dakota, Wyoming, and Montana. The sample was disproportionately weighted toward the West, with nearly half (49%) of the respondents from California and almost a third (27%) coming from the Northeastern states—New York, New Jersey, Pennsylvania, Connecticut, Rhode Island, Massachusetts, Maryland, and New Hampshire.

Most of the respondents (61%) were between ages 30-49, with another 28% between 50-64. Most (70%) were married or partnered, and three-quarters (76%) had at least one child, most of whom (73%) were under age eighteen. Our sample was very well educated (65% with graduate degrees) and had high-status jobs (70% in professional occupations). Still, nearly a third (29%) had incomes below $50,000. Of the respondents who identified themselves as people of color, 29% were black, 17% were Asian (not including the 1% South Asian), 10% were Latino/a, and 40% were of mixed parentage, with white/black being the most common racial mix (15%).

Altogether, these sources produced thousands of pages of qualitative data to support the mailed survey. The various methodologies reinforced each other; the findings and themes were consistent from methodology to methodology.

Foreword

1. For a fascinating autobiographical essay from an Ashkenazi leftist philosopher that ironically reveals many similarities between his experience of Jews in Montreal, Canada, and the story and critical reflections related here—that is, Jewish identity and politics—see G.A. Cohen's "Politics and Religion in a Montreal Communist Jewish Childhood," in his Gifford lectures, *If You're an Egalitarian, How Come You're So Rich?* (Cambridge, MA: Harvard University Press, 2000), 20–41. Cohen, for instance, consistently differentiates between Jews and "pure whites," "lily whites," and he argues that although following the religion of Judaism is sufficient for being a Jew, it is not necessary for being such.

2. See, Claudia Roden, *The Book of Jewish Food: An Odyssey from Samarkand to New York* (New York: Alfred A. Knopf, 1997). This collective memory also speaks to Jews all over the world through the binding force of food. Roden's recipes are prefaced by stories of racially and ethnically diverse Jews from all over the world that provide one of the more accurate tapestries of the Jewish people in print. And the recipes are wonderful.

3. "(1) YAH is the Moon deity as Thoth, Khonsu, or Osiris. (2) WAH means 'to grow' or 'increase.' HAY-WAH is the 'increasing Moon," i.e., Osiris, the New Moon who increases to fullness," Charles S. Finch III, *Echoes of the Old Darkland: Themes from the African Eden* (Decatur, GA: Khenti, Inc., 1991), 161.

4. Marcia Falk, ed., *The Book of Blessings: New Jewish Prayers for Daily Life, the Sabbath, and the New Moon Festival,* (Boston: Beacon Press, 1996), 412.

A Synonym for Jewish

1. Names have been changed to preserve the privacy of the individuals whose stories appear in this book. Unless otherwise noted, quotes are from personal interviews, focus groups, email correspondence, and mail-in survey responses, conducted by the Institute for Jewish & Community Research between 2000-2004.

2. Gary A. Tobin and Sid Groeneman, *Surveying the Jewish Population in the United States - Part 1: Population Estimate, Part 2: Methodological Issues & Challenges* (San Francisco: Institute for Jewish & Community Research, 2004). For more information on this publication, see http://www.jewishresearch.org/publications.htm#jewish. See also Barry A. Kosmin, et al, *Highlights of the CJF 1990 National Jewish Population Survey* (New York: Council of Jewish Federations, 1991); National Jewish Population Survey 2000-01. (New York: United Jewish

Communities, 2003); and United States Census Bureau, Census 2000 Summary File 3 (SF3)—Sample Data, PCT10. "Age by language spoken at home for the population 5 years and over," http://www.census.gov.

3. A study by the Institute for Jewish & Community Research indicates that 26% of Americans raised with two or more religions grow up to become adults with no religious identity at all, while 72% of those raised with no religious identity remain non-identifiers as adults. For more on this phenomenon, see Sid Groeneman and Gary A. Tobin, *The Decline of Religious Identity in the United States* (San Francisco: Institute for Jewish & Community Research, 2004).

4. Egon Mayer, Barry A. Kosmin and Ariela Keysar. *American Religious Identification Survey*, 2001 (New York: The Graduate Center of the City University of New York, 2001).

Describing the Tapestry

1. The United Jews of Color describe themselves as being "dedicated to finding and sharing ways to contradict monolithic images of Jews and Judaism." For more information about this group, see, United Jews of Color, "What Did United Jews of Color Do?," http://members.aol.com/moresheteldad/unitedjewsofcolor.html.

Racial and Religious Change in America

1. United States Census Bureau, "Domestic Migration Across Regions, Divisions, and States: 1995 to 2000," Census 2000 Special Reports, August 2003, http://www.census.gov/prod/2003pubs/censr-7.pdf.

2. Rachel F. Moran, *Interracial Intimacy: The Regulation of Race and Romance* (Chicago: University of Chicago Press, 2003), 19. Interracial relationships have been part of the American experience since the earliest days of the colonies. The earliest anti-miscegenation laws dates from Maryland in 1661.

3. Robert Wuthnow, *After Heaven: Spirituality in America since the 1950s* (Berkeley: University of California Press, 1988) and Wade Clark Roof, *Spiritual Marketplace: Baby Boomers and the Remaking of American Religion* (Princeton: Princeton University Press, 1999).

4. Groeneman and Tobin, *Decline of Religious Identity*.

5. Groeneman and Tobin, *Decline of Religious Identity*.

6. Steven M. Cohen and Arnold M. Eisen, *The Jew Within: Self, Family, and Community in America* (Bloomington, IN: Indiana University Press,

2000). The population surveyed in Cohen and Eisen's study is significantly more Jewishly affiliated than the general Jewish population.

7. For more on the exceptional character of Americans, including American Jews, see Alexander C. Karp, Gary A. Tobin, and Aryeh K. Weinberg, "An Exceptional Nation: American Philanthropy is Different Because America is Different," *Philanthropy* 18, no. 6 (November/December 2004): 2-7.

Jewish Diversity In America and the Politics of Race

1. Karen Zack, *Thinking about Race* (Belmont, CA: Wadsworth Publishing Company, 1998), 2.

2. Zack, *Thinking about Race.*

3. Zack, *Thinking about Race.*

4. Matthew Frye Jacobson, *Whiteness of a Different Color: European Immigrants and the Alchemy of Race* (Cambridge, MA: Harvard University Press, 1998).

5. Lewis Gordon, "African American Jews: An Existential and Historical Portrait" (Lecture, University of California, Berkeley, CA, April 22, 2004).

6. Karen Brodkin, *How Jews Became White Folks and What That Says about Race in America* (New Brunswick, NJ: Rutgers University Press, 1998), 37–39.

7. For further discussion about Jews and whiteness, see Sander Gilman, "Are Jews White? Or, the History of the Nose Job," Chapter 7 in *The Jew's Body* (New York: Routledge, 1991).

8. Brodkin, *How Jews Became White,* 159.

12. Sylvia Barack Fishman, *Double or Nothing? Jewish Families and Mixed Marriage* (Hanover, NH: University Press of New England for Brandeis University Press, 2004).

10. Gary A. Tobin and Katherine G. Simon, *Rabbis Talk about Intermarriage* (San Francisco: Institute for Jewish & Community Research, 1999), 17–22. Among others who have written about the topic are Alan M. Dershowitz, *The Vanishing American Jew: In Search of Jewish Identity for the Next Century* (Boston: Little, Brown, 1997); Elliott Abrams, *Faith or Fear: How Jews Can Survive in a Christian America* (New York: Free Press, 1997); and Paul Cowan with Rachel Cowan, *Mixed Blessings: Marriage between Jews and Christians* (New York: Doubleday, 1987).

11. Peter Y. Medding, Gary A. Tobin, Sylvia Barack Fishman, and Mordechai Rimor, "Jewish Identity in Conversionary and Mixed Marriages," in *Jews in America: A Contemporary Reader*, eds. Roberta Rosenberg Farber and Chaim I. Waxman, 226 (Hanover, NH: University Press of New England for Brandeis University Press, 1999).

12. Harold Schulweis and Edward Feinstein serve as rabbis at Congregation Valley Beth Shalom in Encino, CA. Both Schulweis and Feinstein have been leaders in promoting growth and inclusiveness in the Jewish community.

13. Steven Bayme, "Jewish Organizational Response to Intermarriage," in *Jews in America: A Contemporary Reader*, eds. Farber and Waxman, 151.

14. Bayme, "Organizational Response to Intermarriage," 156.

15. Ami Eden, "Conservative Body Extends Hand to the Intermarried," *Forward*, September 28, 2001, http://www.forward.com/issues/2001/01.09.28/news8.html.

16. National Jewish Outreach Program, http://www.NJOP.org/.

17. Chabad-Lubavitch, http://www.chbad.org/.

18. Union for Reform Judaism, http://URJ.org/.

19. Hebrew Union College-Jewish Institute on Religion, http://huc.edu/libcenters/edprojects.shtml.

20. Jewish Outreach Institute, http://www.joi.org/.

The Last Taboo: Interracial Marriage

1. As a result of the efforts of the Institute for Jewish & Community's Be'chol Lashon Initiative for racially and ethnically diverse Jews, Ruth has found her way back to the Jewish community. She is now a regular and avid participant in Be'chol Lashon events.

2. Katya Gibel Azoulay, *Black, Jewish, and Interracial: It's Not the Color of Your Skin, but the Race of Your Kin, and Other Myths of Identity* (Durham, NC: Duke University Press, 1997).

Feet in Many Rivers: Navigating Multiple Identities

1. Julius Lester, *Lovesong: Becoming a Jew* (New York: Arcade Publishing, 1988).

2. Susan Katz Miller, "The Autograph Man: A Novel about Growing Up with a Jewish Mother and a Chinese Father," InterfaithFamily.com Web Magazine, no. 134 (2004), http://www.interfaithfamily.com/site/apps/nl/content2.asp?c=ekLSK5MLIrG&b=297398&ct=412909.

3. Lise Funderburg, *Black, White, Other: Biracial Americans Talk About Race and Identity* (New York: William Morrow, 1994), 54–58.

4. Funderburg, *Black, White, Other*, 245–46.

5. Quoted in trailer for *Judaism and Race in America*, directed by Avishai Yeganyahu Mekonen and Shari Rothfarb Mekonen, to be released 2006.

Jews Have Always Been Diverse

1. Ephraim Isaac, "The Question of Jewish Identity & Ethiopian Jewish Origins" (Keynote address, Society of Ethiopian Jewish Studies, Addis Ababa, Ethiopia, October 14, 2004).

2. Avi Beker, ed., *Jewish Communities of the World* (Minneapolis: Lerner Publications Company, Institute of the World Jewish Congress, 1998); and World Jewish Congress, "World Jewish Communities," http://www.worldjewishcongress.org/communities/world.cfm.

3. Tobin and Groeneman, *Surveying the Jewish Population*.

4. Israeli Central Bureau of Statistics, "Population, by Population Group," *Monthly Bulletin of Statistics*, July 2005, http://www.cbs.gov.il/yarhon/b1_e.htm.

5. Roden, *Book of Jewish Food*, 3, 9–11.

6. Mavis Hyman, *Indian-Jewish Cooking* (London: Hyman Publishers, 1992), 14.

7. Jewish Virtual Library, "The Spanish Expulsion, 1492," http://www.jewishvirtuallibrary.org/jsource/Judaism/expulsion.html.

8. Jewish Virtual Library, "The Spanish Expulsion, 1492."

9. Jewish Globe, "Sephardim," http://www.jewishglobe.com/Morocco/Sephardic.html.

10. Michael Freund, "Jewish Outreach in Peru," *Israel National News*, January 2, 2005, http://www.israelnationalnews.com/news.php3?id=74588.

11. Nationmaster.com, "Mizrahi Jews," http://www.nationmaster.com/encyclopedia/Mizrahi-Jew.

12. Before the Common Era is a widely-accepted nonsectarian way to refer to B.C. or Before Christ.

13. JIMENA, "Who are the Jews of the Middle East and North Africa?" http://www.jimena-justice.org/faq/faq.htm.

14. Justice for Jews From Arab Countries (JJAC) is a coalition of Jewish communal organizations operating under the auspices of the Conference of Presidents of Major American Jewish Organizations, the American Sephardi Federation, the World Organization of Jews from Arab Countries (WOJAC), in partnership with the American Jewish Committee, American Jewish Congress, Anti-Defamation League, B'nai Brith International, the Jewish Council for Public Affairs and the World Sephardic Congress.

15. Jack Epstein, "Jews who fled Arab lands now press their cause," *San Francisco Chronicle*, March 28, 2004.

16. Marina Benjamin, "Letter from Baghdad: Remnants of Babylonian Jewry Endure Tyranny of the Majority," *Forward*, May 14, 2004.

17. *Jewish Post*, "Justice for Jews from Arab Countries," http://www.jewishpost.com/jp1004/jpn1004k.htm. Despite JJAC's optimism, a June 30, 2005 draft of the new Iraqi constitution contained a clause in Article 1 of the proposed Bill of Rights that specifically excludes an individual with Israeli nationality from either becoming a naturalized Iraqi citizen or holding dual Israeli/Iraqi citizenship. No other nationality is thus singled out for exclusion. For more on this issue and a translation of the draft Bill of Rights, see Nathan J. Brown, "Constitution of Iraq: Draft Bill of Rights," *Carnegie Endowment for International Peace*, http://www.iraqfoundation.org/projects/constitution/BillofRights.pdf.

18. Semha Alwaya, "The Vanishing Jews of the Arab World," *San Francisco Chronicle*, March 6, 2005.

19. Philip Carmel, "Eye on Future, French Group Works for Jewish Refugees from Arab Lands," *Jewish Telegraphic Agency* Email Edition, September 24, 2004.

20. Ephraim Isaac, "Judaism and Islam in Yemen: A Case Study in Historical and Cultural Interaction," *Midstream*, November, 2003, http://www.findarticles.com/p/articles/mi_go1906/is_200311/ai_n6649420.

21. Stanley Mann, "Yemen: A Land of Pure Dreams," *Hagshama*, August 17,2003, http://www.wzo.org.il/en/resources/view.asp?id=1472.

22. Isaac, "Question of Jewish Identity."

23. George E. Lichtblau, "Jewish Roots in Africa," http://kulanu.org/africa/africa2.html.

24. The Talmud is a collection of oral laws (Mishna) and commentary (Gemara) compiled from 200-500 C.E. Torah-based Judaism uses only written law from the Torah as its foundation and not the later texts.

25. Nathan Ausubel, *Pictorial History of the Jewish People, from Bible Times to Our Own Day Throughout the World* (New York: Crown Publishers, 1953), 217.

26. Lawrence J. Epstein, "In Search of the Ten Lost Tribes," *Innernet Magazine*, http://innernet.org.il/article.php?aid=174.

27. Dalia Dabbous, "Few Jews Left in Egypt to Mark First Exodus," Religion News Service, 2003, http://www.hsje.org/few_jews_left_in_egypt_to_mark_f.htm.

28. Michael S. Arnold, "Caught between Arabia and the West, Morocco cultivates its allies with care," *Jewish Telegraphic Agency*, March 16, 2004 and Michael S. Arnold, "For Morocco's Jews, a mixture of integration, vibrancy and decline," *Jewish Telegraphic Agency*, March 16, 2004.

29. PR News Now, "Death of the Grand Rabbi of Tunisia," December 10, 2004, http://www.prnewsnow.com/PR%20News%20Releases/Religion/Islam/Death%20of%20the%20Grand%20Rabbi%20of%20Tunisia.

30. World Jewish Congress, "Algeria," http://www.worldjewishcongress.org/communities/world/middleeast/algeria.cfm.

31. Jewish Virtual Library, "The History of Ethiopian Jews," http://www.jewishvirtuallibrary.org/jsource/Judaism/ejhist.html; Uriel Heilman, "Ethiopian Aliya Cap Threatened," *The Jerusalem Post*, May, 2005; and Falash Mura Tab Listed, *Jewish Telegraphic Agency* Email Edition, May 11, 2005. For more information, see also the North American Conference on Ethiopian Jewry (NACOEJ), http://www.nacoej.org/.

32. Messianic Jews, including the movement "Jews for Jesus," believe that Jesus, whom they call by the Hebrew name "Yeshua," is the messiah, yet they maintain their "Jewish identity." They accept both the Hebrew Bible and the New Testament as the word of God. Messianic Jews proselytize widely among the Jewish community, including among African peoples who have some degree of Jewish identity. They are also very active in the former Soviet Union. The Jewish community does not view them as Jews, nor are they part of any organized Christian denomination.

33. Rudo Mathivha, "The Story of the Lemba People," http://www.haruth.com/JewishLemba.html (Lecture, Zionist Lunch Club, Johannesburg, South Africa, October 15, 1999).

34. Tudor Parfitt, *Journey to the Vanished City: The Search for a Lost Tribe of Israel* (New York: Vintage Departures, 2000), 344-353 and PBS, "The Lemba, the Black Jews of South Afica," http://www.pbs.org/wgbh/nova/israel/familylemba.html. Starting in the mid-1990s, several people, including Trefor Jenkins, Ph.D, at Wits University (Johannesburg), David Goldstein, Ph.D., at Oxford University, and Mark Thomas, Ph.D., at

University College (London), tested the DNA of the Lemba people of South Africa to see if their blood could provide scientific support for the oral tradition that they had migrated from Judea beginning around 500 B.C.E.

35. Rabson Wuriga, personal communication with the author, February 20, 2005.

36. Arye Oded, "A History of the Abayudaya Jews of Uganda," *Jewish Virtual Library*, http://www.jewishvirtuallibrary.org/jsource/Judaism/uganda1.html.

37. Henry Lubega, "Abayudaya - Mbale's Jews," *New Vision*, January 26, 2002.

38. Remy Ilona, "The Ibo Benei-Yisrael Jews of Nigeria," email to Ibo Benei-Yisrael Association of Nigeria list, February 16, 2003, http://groups.yahoo.com/group/ibo-benei-yisrael/?yguid=11539905.

39. Adapted from Jay Sand, "The Jews of Africa," http://www.mindspring.com/~jaypsand/ and Mara Weiss, "Ghana," *Jewish Virtual Library*, http://www.jewishvirtuallibrary.org/jsource/vjw/ghana.html.

40. Adapted from Sand, "The Jews of Africa."

41. Adapted from Sand, "The Jews of Africa" and M. Mitchell Serels, "An Unusual Society in Cape Verde," Kulanu, http://www.kulanu.org/cape-verde/capeverde.html.

42. Adapted from Sand, "The Jews of Africa" and Yitzchak Kerem, "Portuguese Crypto-Jews," *Saudades*, http://www.saudades.org/portcrypto.html.

43. Romiel Daniel, "The Jews of India" (working paper, Be'chol Lashon Think Tank, San Francisco, February 18, 2005).

44. Aharon Daniel, "Cochini Jews of Kerala," http://adaniel.tripod.com/cochin.htm.

45. Aharon Daniel, "Baghdadi Jews in India," http://adaniel.tripod.com/baghdadi.htm.

46. Shalva Weil, "The Bene Israel of India," *Museum of the Jewish People*, http://www.bh.org.il/Communities/Archive/BeneIsrael.asp.

47. Dan Pine, "A tribe of Many Colors," *J. The Jewish News Weekly of Northern California (formerly The Jewish Bulletin of Northern California)*, February 25, 2005.

48. Nationmaster.com, "Judaism in India," http://www.nationmaster.com/encyclopedia/Judaism-in-India.

49. B'nei Menashe, http://www.bneimenashe.com/.

50. IsraelNationalNews.com, "Rabbinate Recognizes B'nei Menashe as 'Descendants of Israel,'" April 3, 2005, http://israelnationalnews.com/news.php3?id=79370.

51. Zev Chafets, "The Rabbi Who Loved Evangelicals (and Vice Versa)," *New York Times*, July 24, 2005.

52. Michael Pollack, "The Jews of Kaifeng," *Sino-Judaic Institute*, http://www.sino-judaic.org/kaifeng.html.

53. Xu Xin, "Jews in Kaifeng, China: A Brief History,"Nanjing University, November, 2003. For more informaton, see Xu Xin and Beverly Friend, *Legends of the Chinese Jews of Kaifeng* (Hoboken, NJ: KTAV Publishing House, 1995); Xu Xin, *The Jews of Kaifeng, China: History, Culture, and Religion* (Hoboken, NJ: KTAV Publishing House, 2003); China Judaic Studies Association, http://www.oakton.edu/~friend/chinajews.html; Chabad Shanghai Jewish Center, http://www.chinajewish.org/; and Kehillat Beijing Jewish Community, http://www.sinogogue.org/.

54. Sheridan Prasso, "Salvaging Jewish Heritage in China, Block by Block," *New York Times*. May 31, 2004.

55. Mark Magnier, "A Home for Jews in China," *Los Angeles Times*, September 22, 2004. For more information, see Irena Vladimirsky, "The Jews of Harbin," *Database of Jewish Communities*, http://www.bh.org.il/Communities/Archive/Harbin.asp and Igud Yotzei Sin (Association of Former Residents of China in Israel), http://www.jewsofchina.org/.

56. Sino-Judaic Institute, http://www.sino-judaic.org.

57. For example, Yochanan Bwejeri, president of Havila Institute in Brussels, advocates on behalf of the Tutsis or Batutsis in Rwanda and Burundi whose oral traditions teach that they are the descendants of the Israelite tribes of Judah and Dan. For more information, see Yochanan Bwejeri, "Havila and the Tutsi Hebrews," *Kulanu*, http://www.kulanu.org/africa/havila.html or contact institut_de_havila@yahoo.fr.

58. Ken Blady, *Jewish Communities in Exotic Places* (Northvale, NJ: Jason Aronson, 2000).

59. Alexandra J. Wall, "Jews Caught Blue-Handed in Book on Exotic Rituals," *J. The Jewish News Weekly of Northern California (formerly The Jewish Bulletin of Northern California)*, June 23, 2000, http://www.jewishsf.com/bk000623/ebaexotic.shtml.

60. Kulanu is a non-profit organization "dedicated to finding lost and dispersed remnants of Jewish people and assisting those who wish to rejoin the Jewish community." For more information on Kulanu, see their website: http://kulanu.org/about-kulanu/about-us.html.

61. Karen Primack, "Irony" in Primack, ed., *Jews in Places You Never Thought of* (Hoboken, NJ: KTAV Publishing House, 1998), 288.

62. There are groups throughout the world that are in transition from Christianity to Judaism. Some congregations and communities began as Judaic Christians; they practiced Christianity and adopted some Jewish practices. Over time, they gradually shed their Christian theology, including belief in Jesus as the messiah and became Jewish in belief and practice. Even those that may no longer have any Christian identification or practice may have vestiges of their Christian origins, such as the use of the title "pastor" or "overseer." It is expected that these last trappings of Christianity will fade away over time. These include groups in Cameroon for example, as well as congregations throughout the United States. The Jewish community is understandably suspicious of such groups but would be better served by better understanding the continuum of transformation to Judaism.

63. Isaac, "Question of Jewish Identity."

Who Is a Jew? Ideology and Bloodlines

1. Isaac, "Question of Jewish Identity."

2. Union for Reform Judaism, "Who is a Jew?," http://urj.org/ask/who_jew/.

3. Rabbi Capers Funnye, email to authors, September 29, 2003.

4. Yvonne Chireau and Nathaniel Deutsch, editors of *Black Zion: African American Religious Encounters with Judaism* (New York: Oxford University Press, 2000) and James E. Landing, author of *Black Judaism: Story of an American Movement* (Durham, NC: Carolina Academic Press, 2001) have done work on the history of African Jews in the Americas. This history dates back hundreds of years.

5. Rabbi Sholomo Ben Levy, "General Description of the Black Jewish or Hebrew Israelite Community," *Black Jews, Hebrews, and Israelites*, http://www.blackjews.org/.

6. In addition to Rabbis Capers Funnye and Sholomo Ben Levy, leaders of the Israelite community include Rabbi Hailu Paris, Rabbi Baruch Yehuda, and spiritual leader Debra Bowen. For a list of congregations and rabbis, see Israelite Board of Rabbis, http://www.blackjews.org/.

7. Levy, "Hebrew Israelite Community."

8. The evolution of Black Nationalism into traditional Judaism continues for some, while for others it creates purposeful segregation from white Jews.

By Choice or by Destiny

1. Conversion to Judaism has taken place throughout history. Ruth, an ancestor of King David, was a convert. For more on converts and conversion in Jewish history, see J.R. Rosenbloom, *Conversion to Judaism: From the Biblical Period to the Present* (Cincinnati, OH: Hebrew Union College Press, 1978).

2. Tobin is not alone in advocating for welcoming converts. Others calling for this policy include Lawrence Epstein, president of the Conversion to Judaism Resource Center and author of several scholarly and practical books on conversion, including editing *Readings on Conversion to Judaism* (Northvale, NJ: Jason Aronson, 1995), and Egon Mayer, founder of the Jewish Outreach Institute and author of "Why Not Judaism? Conversion Could Be the Answer to the Interfaith Marriage Problem," *Moment* 16, no.5 (October, 1991): 28–33, 39–42.

3. Gary A. Tobin, *Opening the Gates: How Proactive Conversion Can Revitalize the Jewish Community* (San Francisco: Jossey-Bass, 1999), 90–91.

4. David W. Belin, "Choosing Judaism: An Opportunity for Everyone," *Jewish Outreach Institute*, http://www.joi.org/library/pubs/belin_8.shtml. During the Talmudic period, commencing approximately 2,200 years ago, Jewish missionary efforts were so successful that in the 1ˢᵗ century the world Jewish population increased to between two and five million. However, in the 4ᵗʰ century the Edict of Constantine established Christianity as the official state religion and made conversion to Judaism a capital offense. Conversion efforts therefore ceased but resumed to some degree in medieval times. Then, in the late 15th century when the Spanish Inquisition reinstituted capital punishment for the "crime" of conversion to Judaism, together with a doctrine of "heresy," Jewish conversion efforts ceased and the rabbis developed a tradition of discouraging converts. This post-Inquisition development has led many Jews to assume erroneously that Judaism does not welcome converts, when in fact there have been long periods in Jewish history when Jews actively sought proselytes. In its truest ideals, Judaism is a loving, meaningful religion that welcomes all.

5. Rabbi Manny Viñas, email to authors, November 12, 2004.

6. Isaac, "Question of Jewish Identity."

7. Ben Ami Carter, one of the founders of the Original Hebrew Israelite Nation, or Black Israelites, which was founded in Chicago in the 1960s. The Black Israelites are supporters of the Black Zionism movement. In 1968, a group of Black Israelites flew to Israel and founded several communities in Israel, the most famous in Dimona in the Negev Desert. After years of struggle with the Israeli government for recognition, in 1990 they were granted temporary resident status, and in 2004 that status switched to permanent residency, which does not require military service. Their official status as Jews in Israel remains a matter of controversy. For more information about this group, see, among others, The Black Hebrews, http://www.jewishvirtuallibrary.org/jsource/Society_&_Culture/Black_Hebrews.html.

8. Trailer for *Judaism and Race in America*, directed by Avishai Yeganyahu Mekonen and Shari Rothfarb Mekonen, to be released 2006.

9. Nachum Dershowitz, "Notes from a Friend on Conversion to Judaism," http://www.cs.tau.ac.il/%7Enachumd/sch/sch/conversion.html.

10. Dershowitz, "Conversion to Judaism."

11. Dershowitz, "Conversion to Judaism."

12. Barack Fishman, *Double or Nothing?*

13. For more on this line of thinking regarding conversion, see Jonathan D. Sarna, "Reform Jewish Leaders, Intermarriage, and Conversion." In Lawrence J. Epstein, ed., *Readings on Conversion to Judaism* (1995) and Jack Wertheimer, Charles S. Leibman, and Steven M. Cohen, "How to Save American Jews," *Commentary*, 101, no.1 (1996): 47–51.

14. Tobin, *Opening the Gates*, 29.

15. Tobin, *Opening the Gates*, 147–163. Numerous books have been published to assist converts. They include Anita Diamant, *Choosing a Jewish Life: A Handbook for People Converting to Judaism and for Their Family and Friends* (New York: Schocken Books, 1997); and Allan L. Berkowitz and Patti Moscovitz, eds., *Embracing the Covenant: Converts to Judaism Talk about Why and How* (Woodstock, VT: Jewish Lights Publishing, 1996).

16. For more information, see the following web sites on conversion to Judaism, http://www.convert.org/ and http://www.convertingtojudaism.com/.

And for Those Too Young to Ask: Transracial Adoption

1. Naomi Pfefferman, "The Adoption Challenge," *The Jewish Journal*, October 23, 1998, http://www.jewishjournal.com/home/searchview.php?id=5095.

2. Yilu Zhao, "Living in Two Worlds, Old and New: Foreign-Born Adoptees Explore Their Cultural Roots," *The New York Times*, April 9, 2002.

3. Joseph Crumbley, "Seven Tasks for Parents—Developing Positive Racial Identity," *Adoptive Families*, September/October 1999.

4. Cited in Pfefferman, "The Adoption Challenge."

5. Pfefferman, "The Adoption Challenge."

6. Merry Madway Eisenstadt and Debra Nussbaum Cohen, "Adoption: The 'Changing Face of the Jewish Community'," *Washington Jewish Week*, February 3, 2000.

7. Peter Hartlaub, "Making a World of Difference," *San Francisco Chronicle*, November 4, 2001.

8. Shelley Kapnek Rosenberg, *Adoption and the Jewish Family: Contemporary Perspectives*, (Philadelphia: Jewish Publication Society, 1998), 2.

9. Rabbi Michael Gold, "Adoption as a Jewish Option," *Adoption.com*, http://library.adoption.com/Jewish-Adoption/Adoption-as-a-Jewish-Option/article/2800/1.html.

10. Gold, "Adoption as a Jewish Option."

11. Gold, "Adoption as a Jewish Option."

Patches of Color, Patches of White

1. Johanna Ginsberg, "Newark Shul Shows Face of a Diverse Jewish Future," *New Jersey Jewish News*, February 5, 2004, http://www.njjewishnews.com/njjn.com/2504/mwshul.html.

2. Israelite Board of Rabbis, http://blackjews.org/israelite_board_of_rabbis.htm.

3. Rabbi Manny Viñas, email to authors, November 12, 2004.

Toward a More Inclusive Future

1. Among the grassroots organizations, list servs, and websites devoted to diverse Jews are: Alliance of Black Jews, http://www.aobj.org/;

KULANU, http://www.kulanu.org/; Ayecha, http://www.ayecha.org/; The Jewish Multicultural Network, http://www.isabellafreedman.org/jmn/jmn_intro.shtml; Moreshet Network of Jews of Afrikan Heritages, http://www.moreshetnetwork.com/; Black American Jews, http://www.blackandjewish.com/; Black and Jewish Web Page, http://www.angelfire.com/ca/dorseydon/; Jews in Africa, http://www.mindspring.com/~jaypsand/; Afram Jews, http://groups.yahoo.com/group/aframjews/; and http://rabbihowardgorin.org/.

2. "Building Bridges between Communities of Jews" Workshop, (Be'chol Lashon Think Tank, San Francisco, January 19, 2004).

3. Institute for Jewish & Community Research, "Be'chol Lashon Newsletter," http://www.JewishResearch.org/socialchange.htm#becholupdates.

4. Jewish Outreach Institute, "Jewish Outreach Scan of the San Francisco Bay Area" (New York, NY, April 2005).

5. "Building Bridges" Workshop.

Who Is a Jew, Really?
1. James R. Ross, *Fragile Branches: Travels Through the Jewish Diaspora* (New York: Riverhead Books, 2000), 225.

aliyah (Hebrew; **aliyot** - pl.) – Literally, "going up, ascending." (1) The honor of being called up to recite a blessing before the reading of the Torah portion; (2) immigration to Israel.

Anusim (Hebrew; also, **Anousim** and **Bnei Anousim**) – Literally, "the coerced." Jews whose ancestors were forced to convert to Catholicism in Spain and Portugal over 500 years ago.

Ashkenazi – Jews who derive from northern Europe and who generally follow the customs originating in medieval German Judaism. By extension, it also refers to Jews of eastern European background (including Russia) with their distinctive liturgical practices or religious and social customs.

bar or **bat mitzvah** (Hebrew) – Literally, "The child responsible for fulfilling the commandments." The term used to describe the thirteen-year-old child (or sometimes twelve-year-old girl) who celebrates this occasion by reading from the Torah and Haftorah during the Saturday morning service. (bar = boy, bat = girl)

beit din (Hebrew) – Three-person rabbinic court, guided by the principles of halakha. May be convened for the purpose of overseeing a conversion ceremony, to prepare a Jewish writ of divorce, or to serve as a mediating body in a dispute between two Jews.

bima (Hebrew) – (1) The dais in a sanctuary from which the Torah is read and where the leader of the service stands when leading services; (2) the front platform of a synagogue where the ark containing the Torah stands. Also called "tebah" in Sephardic communities.

brit milah (Hebrew; also, **bris** - Yiddish) – Ritual circumcision of male children at eight days old symbolizing the covenant between God and Abraham.

challah – A portion of bread set aside from the main bread for ritual purposes. May be any type of bread, and in Ashkenazi tradition, usually an egg bread, often braided, eaten during Shabbat and on Jewish holidays.

Chanukah (also, **Hanukkah**) – The eight-day Festival of Lights, commemorating both the miracle of the Maccabees, whose oil lasted for 8 days, and their victory over Greco-Syrian religious oppression and the subsequent rededication of the temple in Jerusalem. Usually falls in December.

chanukiah (Hebrew; also, **hanukkiah**) – A nine-branched menorah used at Chanukah.

Chueta (Catalan) – A derogatory term meaning "swine" used to describe Jews forced to convert to Catholicism on the Spanish island of Mallorca over 500 years ago.

chupah (also, **huppah**) – Jewish marriage canopy.

Converso – Jews forced to convert to Catholicism on the Iberian Peninsula over 500 years ago. Many Conversos secretly continued to practice Judaism or retained some Jewish customs.

crypto-Jew – Literally, "hidden Jew." Jews forced to convert to another religion who secretly practiced Judaism. Most often applied to Iberian Conversos but also applicable to other groups of Jews throughout history.

daven (Yiddish) – To pray.

ger (Hebrew; **gerim** - pl.) – A convert.

ger toshav (Hebrew) – Literally, "fellow traveler." Partial proselyte or someone who has not formally converted to Judaism.

gerut (Hebrew) – Conversion.

goy (Yiddish; **goyim** - pl.) – Literally, "other." Used to describe non-Jewish people. Derived from the Hebrew word for "nation."

halakha (Hebrew) – Literally, "the path." Scriptural laws; a generic term for the whole legal system of Judaism.

halakhic – According to scriptural law.

Hashem (Hebrew) – Literally, "the Name." A name for God, used by those who do not want to take God's Hebrew name "in vain."

Havdalah – The ceremony which ends the Sabbath. Benedictions are recited over wine, a candle, and spices. Different customs prevail in various communities; a lighted candle is usually extinguished in the wine. The ceremony reputedly stems from the days of the Great Synagogue.

havurah (Hebrew; **havurot** - pl.) – Literally, "community." A group or fellowship organized around prayer, study, celebration of Jewish holidays, spiritual and/or social purposes.

Hillel – Jewish organization that serves college and university students on campuses.

Kabbalah – A thread of Jewish mysticism that includes speculation on divinity, creation, and the fate of the soul and consists of meditative, devotional, and mystical practices. Considered an esoteric offshoot of Judaism.

Kaddish – Prayer for the dead.

kashrut – The Jewish dietary laws.

kehillah (Hebrew) – Community.

kiddush – The blessing over wine for meals, Shabbat, festivals, and holy days.

kippah (Hebrew; **kippot** - pl.) – Skullcap traditionally worn by Jewish males, also used by some Jewish females, representing the hand of God.

kiruv (Hebrew; also, **keruv**) – Literally, "to draw near." Encouragement for mixed-married families to maintain their Jewish ties. Also, any movement to attract Jews to increased religious observance.

Kohan (**Kohanim** - pl.) – A descendant of Aaron, Moses' brother, and a member of the priestly class.

kreplach (Yiddish) – Triangular dumplings of Eastern European origin usually filled with meat, onions, and potatoes, served on Jewish holidays.

kosher – Prepared in accordance with Jewish dietary laws (kashrut), most often referring to food.

L'shanah tovah (Hebrew) – Literally, "For a good year." A traditional greeting on Rosh Hashonah, the Jewish New Year.

mamzer (Hebrew) – Bastard.

Marrano (Spanish) – A derogatory term meaning "swine" applied to Spanish Jews forced to convert to Catholicism over 500 years ago.

menorah – The seven-branched candlestick that stood in the Tabernacle and in the Jerusalem Temple. According to Exodus, its pattern was a divine gift to Moses.

meshummad (Hebrew) – An apostate, one who voluntarily abandons his or her religious faith.

Midrash – Rabbinic commentaries to the Torah.

mikveh (Hebrew; also, **mikvah**; **mikvot** - pl.) – A ritual bath used for purification purposes by married women after menstruation, by brides before nuptials, and by converts at the culmination of the conversion ceremony.

minyan (Hebrew) – Quorum of ten Jewish adults necessary for a public prayer service. The minyan represents the Jewish people as a community.

mitzvah (Hebrew; **mitzvot** -pl.) – A commandment, positive or negative; one of the 613 Torah-given precepts or one of the rabbinic commandments added later; also loosely refers to a "good deed."

Mizrahi - Jews of Middle Eastern origin; Jewish communities indigenous to the Middle East.

New Christian – A term applied specifically to three groups of Jewish converts to Christianity and their descendants in the Iberian Peninsula. The first group converted following the massacres in Spain in 1391. The second, also in Spain, were baptized following the decree of Fernando and Isabel in 1492 expelling all Jews who refused to accept Christianity. The third group, in Portugal, were converted by force and royal fiat in 1497.

Oneg Shabbat (Hebrew) – Literally, "Sabbath joy." A celebration following Friday evening services that may include refreshments, singing, and dancing.

Pesach (Passover) – The holiday celebrating the Exodus of the Israelites from Egypt.

Rosh Hashonah – The Jewish New Year.

Seder (Hebrew) – Literally, "order." Ritual meal at Passover.

Sephardi (Hebrew; **Sephardim** - pl.) – Literally, "Spanish." From the Hebrew word "Sepharad," meaning "Spain." Refers to Jews descended from those who lived on the Iberian Peninsula before the expulsion of 1492. As a cultural designation, the term refers to Iberian Jews who settled in North Africa, the Balkans, and the Middle East. (See also Ashkenazi and Mizrahi.)

Shabbat (Hebrew; also, **Shabbos** - Yiddish) – The Sabbath, the day of rest; the seventh day of the week. Begins at sundown Friday and ends at sundown on Saturday.

Shabbaton – Sabbath retreat.

Shavuot – Literally, "weeks." Feast of the Weeks; the festival celebrating the Spring harvest season, which is held exactly seven weeks after Passover; also commemorates the anniversary of the giving of the Ten Commandments to Moses and the Israelites at Mount Sinai.

shiva (Hebrew) – Days of mourning following a death.

Sh'ma – Jewish prayer that is the principle statement of faith and belief affirming that there is one God.

shtetl (Yiddish) – A Jewish small town in Eastern Europe.

shul (Yiddish) – Synagogue.

Siddur (**Siddurim** - pl.) – The Jewish prayerbook.

simcha (Hebrew) –A joyous occasion.

sukkah – Huts or outdoor shelters built during Sukkot, the harvest festival.

Sukkot – Feast of the Tabernacles; one of the three ancient harvest and pilgrimage festivals (with Pesach and Shavuot); the thanksgiving and harvest holiday that occurs five days after Yom Kippur.

synagogue – House of worship.

tallit (Hebrew; also **tallis** - Yiddish) – A ritual prayer shawl.

Talmud – A compilation of rabbinic teachings, comprising the Mishna (oral laws) and the Gemara (commentary on the laws).

Tanach (also, **Tanakh**) – An acronym for Torah (the five books of Moses), Nevi'im (Prophets), and Ketuvim (writings) used to describe a body of Jewish religious texts.

tashlich (Hebrew) – Literally, "to send, to cast out." The special ceremony on Rosh Hashonah afternoon in which Jews symbolically cast their sins (in the form of bread crumbs) into a body of flowing water.

tefillin (Hebrew) – Known in English as "phylacteries," leather boxes and straps containing the four biblical passages of the Sh'ma; wrapped around the arm and on the forehead in accordance with Deuteronomy 6:4-9 and 11:13-21.

tinoq shenishba (Hebrew) – A child taken captive and raised as a non-Jew.

Torah – (1) The five books of Moses; (2) the sacred texts of Judaism.

tikkun olam (Hebrew) – Literally, "To repair the world." In Jewish teaching, one is expected to "repair the world" daily through both deed and thought.

yahrtzeit (Yiddish) – Literally, "anniversary." The anniversary of the Jewish calendar date of someone's death.

yarmulke – Skull cap. (See also kippah.)

yeshiva – Jewish school of religious instruction.

Yisrael (Hebrew) – Literally, "Israel." In a religious context, refers to the majority of Jews who are neither Kohanim nor members of the tribe of Levi. Also, Eretz Yisrael is the "Land of Israel."

Yom Kippur – Day of Atonement; the holiest day of the Jewish religious year, the last day of the Ten Days of Penitence. A fast day, during which Jews seeks forgiveness for sins.

Yom Tov – Holiday.

Selected Bibliography

Abrams, Elliott. *Faith or Fear: How Jews Can Survive in a Christian America*. New York: Free Press, 1997.

Agosín, Marjorie, ed. *Miriam's Daughters: Jewish Latin American Women Poets*. Bilingual ed. Santa Fe: Sherman Asher Publishing, 2001.

Alexander, Michael. *Jazz Age Jews*. Princeton, NJ: Princeton University Press, 2001.

Alperson, Myra. *Dim Sum, Bagels and Grits: A Sourcebook for Multicultural Families*. New York: Farrar, Straus and Giroux, 2001.

Appiah, K. Anthony, and Amy Gutmann. *Color Conscious: The Political Morality of Race*. Princeton, NJ: Princeton University Press, 1996.

Arboleda, Teja. *In the Shadow of Race: Growing up as a Multiethnic, Multicultural, and "Multiracial" American*. Mahwah, NJ: Lawrence Erlbaum Associates Publishers, 1998.

Azoulay, Katya Gibel. *Black, Jewish and Interracial: It's Not the Color of Your Skin, but the Race of Your Kin, and Other Myths of Identity*. Durham, NC: Duke University Press, 1997.

Back, Les, and John Solomos, eds. *Theories of Race and Racism: A Reader*. London: Routledge, 2000.

Baker, Lee D. *From Savage to Negro: Anthropology and the Construction of Race, 1896-1954.* Berkeley: University of California Press, 1998.

Banton, Michael. *Ethnic and Racial Consciousness*. 2nd ed. London: Addison Wesley Longman, 1997.

Bard, Mitchell G. *From Tragedy to Triumph: The Politics Behind the Rescue of Ethiopian Jewry*. Westport, CT: Praeger, 2002.

Beker, Avi, ed. *Jewish Communities of the World*. Minneapolis: Lerner Publications Company, Institute of the World Jewish Congress, 1998.

Bennett, Lerone, Jr. *Before the Mayflower: A History of Black America*. 6th ed. New York: Penguin Books, 1988.

Berger, Graenum. *Black Jews in America: A Documentary with Commentary*. New York: Commission on Synagogue Relations, Federation of Jewish Philanthropies of New York, 1978.

Berger, Maurice. *White Lies: Race and the Myths of Whiteness*. New York: Farrar, Straus and Giroux, 1999.

Berkowitz, Allan L., and Patti Moscovitz, eds. *Embracing the Covenant: Converts to Judaism Talk About Why and How*. Woodstock, VT: Jewish Lights Publishing, 1996.

Bernal, Martha E., and George P. Knight, eds. *Ethnic Identity: Formation and Transmission among Hispanics and Other Minorities*. Albany: State University of New York Press, 1993.

Bernardini, Paolo, and Norman Fiering, eds. *The Jews and the Expansion of Europe to the West, 1450 to 1800*. 2 vols. New York: Berghahn Books, 2001.

Biale, David, Michael Galchinsky, and Susannah Heschel. *Insider/Outsider: American Jews and Multiculturalism*. Berkeley and Los Angeles: University of California Press, 1998.

Birmingham, Stephen. *The Grandees: America's Sephardic Elite*. Syracuse: Syracuse University Press, 1971.

Blady, Ken. *Jewish Communities in Exotic Places*. Northvale, NJ: Jason Aronson, 2000.

Brodkin, Karen. *How Jews Became White Folks and What That Says About Race in America*. New Brunswick, NJ: Rutgers University Press, 1998.

Brodzinsky, David M., Marshall D. Schechter & Robin Marantz Henig. *Being Adopted: The Lifelong Search for Self*. New York: Anchor Books, 1993.

Brotz, Howard. *The Black Jews of Harlem: Negro Nationalism and the Dilemmas of Negro Leadership, Sourcebooks in Negro History*. New York: Schocken Books, 1964.

Chideya, Farai. *The Color of Our Future: Race for the 21ˢᵗ Century*. New York: Quill/William Morrow, 1999.

Chireau, Yvonne, and Nathaniel Deutsch, eds. *Black Zion: African American Religious Encounters with Judaism*. New York: Oxford University Press, 2000.

Chun, Gloria Heyung. *Of Orphans and Warriors: Inventing Chinese American Culture and Identity*. New Brunswick, NJ: Rutgers University Press, 2000.

Cimino, Richard P. and Don Lattin. *Shopping for Faith: American Religion in the New Millennium*. San Francisco: Jossey-Bass, 1998.

Clark, Christine, and James O'Donnell, eds. *Becoming and Unbecoming White: Owning and Disowning a Racial Identity.* Westport, CT: Bergin and Garvey, 1999.

Cohen, Steven M., and Arnold M. Eisen. *The Jew Within: Self, Family, and Community in America.* Bloomington, IN: Indiana University Press, 2000.

Cornell, Stephen, and Douglas Hartmann. *Ethnicity and Race: Making Identities in a Changing World.* Thousand Oaks, CA: Pine Forge Press, 1998.

Cose, Ellis. *Color-Blind: Seeing Beyond Race in a Race-Obsessed World.* New York: Harper Perennial, 1997.

Cowan, Paul, with Rachel Cowan. *Mixed Blessings: Marriage between Jews and Christians.* New York: Doubleday, 1987.

Dalmage, Heather M. *Tripping on the Color Line: Black-White Multiracial Families in a Racially Divided World.* New Brunswick, NJ: Rutgers University Press, 2000.

Delman, Carmit. *Burnt Bread and Chutney: Growing Up between Cultures—a Memoir of an Indian Jewish Girl.* New York: Ballantine Books, 2002.

Derman-Sparks, Louise, and Carol Brunson Phillips. *Teaching/Learning Anti-Racism: A Developmental Approach.* New York: Teachers College Press, Columbia University, 1997.

Dershowitz, Alan M. *The Vanishing American Jew: In Search of Jewish Identity for the Next Century.* Boston: Little, Brown, 1997.

Diamant, Anita. *Choosing a Jewish Life: A Handbook for People Converting to Judaism and for Their Family and Friends.* New York: Schocken Books, 1997.

Epstein, Lawrence J., ed. *Readings on Conversion to Judaism.* Northvale, NJ: Jason Aronson, 1995.

Essed, Philomena, and David Theo Goldberg, eds. *Race Critical Theories: Text and Context.* Malden, MA: Blackwell Publishers, 2002.

Farber, Roberta Rosenberg, and Chaim I. Waxman, eds. *Jews in America: A Contemporary Reader.* Hanover, NH: University Press of New England for Brandeis University Press, 1999.

Fine, Michelle, Lois Weis, Linda C. Powell, and L. Mun Wong, eds. *Off White: Readings on Race, Power, and Society.* New York: Routledge, 1997.

Fishman, Sylvia Barack. *Double or Nothing?: Jewish Families and Mixed Marriage.* Hanover, NH: University Press of New England for Brandeis University Press, 2004.

Fong, Timothy P., and Larry H. Shinagawa, eds. *Asian Americans: Experiences and Perspectives.* Upper Saddle River, NJ: Prentice-Hall, 2000.

Frankenberg, Ruth, ed. *Displacing Whiteness: Essays in Social and Cultural Criticism.* Durham, NC: Duke University Press, 1997.

———. *White Women, Race Matters: The Social Construction of Whiteness.* Minneapolis: University of Minnesota Press, 1993.

Fredrickson, George M. *The Black Image in the White Mind: The Debate on Afro-American Character and Destiny, 1817-1914.* Hanover, NH: Wesleyan University Press, 1971.

———. *Racism: A Short History.* Princeton, NJ: Princeton University Press, 2002.

Friedland, Ronnie, and Edmund Case, eds. *The Guide to Jewish Interfaith Family Life: An Interfaithfamily.Com Handbook.* Woodstock, VT: Jewish Lights Publishing, 2001.

Fry, Ying Ying. *Kids Like Me in China.* St. Paul, MN: Yeong and Yeong Book Company, 2001.

Funderburg, Lise. *Black, White, Other: Biracial Americans Talk About Race and Identity.* New York: William Morrow, 1994.

Gallup, George, Jr., and D. Michael Lindsay. *Surveying the Religious Landscape: Trends in U.S. Beliefs.* Harrisburg, PA: Morehouse Publishing, 1999.

Gaskins, Pearl Fuyo, ed. *What Are You? Voices of Mixed-Race Young People.* New York: Henry Holt and Company, 1999.

Gates, Henry Louis, Jr. *Thirteen Ways of Looking at a Black Man.* New York: Random House, 1997.

Gerchunoff, Alberto. *The Jewish Gauchos of the Pampas.* Translated by Prudencio de Pereda. Albuquerque: University of New Mexico Press, 1998.

Gillespie, Peggy, and Gigi Kaeser. *Of Many Colors: Portraits of Multiracial Families.* Amherst: University of Massachusetts Press, 1997.

Gilman, Sander L., and Milton Shain, eds. *Jewries at the Frontier: Accommodation, Identity, Conflict.* Urbana, IL: University of Illinois Press, 1999.

Gilroy, Paul. *Against Race: Imagining Political Culture Beyond the Color Line*. Cambridge, MA: Belknap Press of Harvard University Press, 2000.

Glaser, Gabrielle. *Strangers to the Tribe: Portraits of Interfaith Marriage*. New York: Houghton Mifflin Company, 1997.

Glazier, Stephen D. *Encyclopedia of African and African-American Religions*. New York: Routledge, 2001.

Goldberg, David Theo, ed. *Multiculturalism: A Critical Reader*. Cambridge, MA: Blackwell Publishers, 1994.

Goldstein, Jonathan, ed. *The Jews of China*. Vol. 1, *Historical and Comparative Perspectives*. Vol. 2, *A Sourcebook and Research Guide*. Armonk, NY: M.E. Sharpe, 1999-2000.

Gonen, Rivka. *To the Ends of the Earth: The Quest for the Ten Lost Tribes of Israel*. Northvale, NJ: Jason Aronson, 2002.

Gordis, David M., and Yoav Ben-Horin, eds. *Jewish Identity in America*. Los Angeles: The Susan and David Wilstein Institute of Jewish Policy Studies, University of Judaism, 1991.

Gordon, Lewis R. *Bad Faith and Antiblack Racism*. Atlantic Highlands, NJ: Humanities Press International, 1995.

———, ed. *Existence in Black: An Anthology of Black Existential Philosophy*. New York: Routledge, 1997.

———. *Existentia Africana: Understanding Africana Existential Thought*. New York: Routledge, 2000.

———. *Her Majesty's Other Children: Sketches of Racism from a Neocolonial Age*. Lanham, MD: Rowman and Littlefield, 1997.

Gordon, Lewis R., T. Denean Sharpley-Whiting, and Renee T. White, eds. *Fanon: A Critical Reader*. Oxford: Blackwell Publishers, 1996.

Gossett, Thomas F. Race: *The History of an Idea in America*. New York: Oxford University Press, 1963.

Graves, Joseph L., Jr. *The Emperor's New Clothes: Biological Theories of Race at the Millenium*. New Brunswick, NJ: Rutgers University Press, 2001.

Gray, Ahuvah. *My Sister, the Jew*. Southfield, MI: Targum Press, 2001.

Groeneman, Sid and Gary Tobin. *The Decline of Religious Identity in the United States*. San Francisco: The Institute for Jewish & Community Research, 2004.

Gunthorpe, Wayne West. *Skin Color Recognition, Preference and Identification in Interracial Children*. Lanham, MD: University Press of America, 1998.

Halkin, Hillel. *Across the Sabbath River: In Search of a Lost Tribe of Israel*. Boston: Houghton Mifflin Company, 2002.

Hall, Christine C. Iijima. *Please Choose One: Ethnic Identity Choices for Biracial Individuals*. Newbury Park, CA: Sage Publications, 1992.

Haney Lopez, Ian F. *White by Law: The Legal Construction of Race*. New York: New York University Press, 1996.

Helms, Janet E., ed. *Black and White Racial Identity: Theory, Research, and Practice*. Westport, CT: Praeger Publishers, 1990.

Herron, Carolivia. *Nappy Hair*. New York: Dragonfly Books / Alfred A. Knopf, 1997.

Hodes, Martha, ed. *Sex, Love, Race: Crossing Boundaries in North American History*. New York: New York University Press, 1999.

Hollinger, David A. *Postethnic America: Beyond Multiculturalism*. New York: BasicBooks, 1995.

Holt, Thomas C. *The Problem of Race in the Twenty-First Century*. Cambridge, MA: Harvard University Press, 2000.

Hyman, Mavis. *Indian-Jewish Cooking*. London: Hyman Publishers, 1992.

Ignatiev, Noel. *How the Irish Became White*. New York: Routledge, 1995.

Israel, Rachael Rukmini. *The Jews of India: Their Story*. New Delhi: Mosaic Books, 2002.

Jackson, Randolph. *Black People in the Bible*. New York: Vantage Press, 2002.

Jacobson, Matthew Frye. *Barbarian Virtues: The United States Encounters Foreign Peoples at Home and Abroad, 1876-1917*. New York: Hill and Wang, 2000.

———. *Whiteness of a Different Color: European Immigrants and the Alchemy of Race*. Cambridge, MA: Harvard University Press, 1998.

Johnson, Kevin R. *How Did You Get to Be Mexican? A White/Brown Man's Search for Identity*. Philadelphia: Temple University Press, 1999.

Kalinsky, George. *Rabbis: The Many Faces of Judaism: 100 Unexpected Photographs of Rabbis with Essays in Their Own Words.* New York: Universe, 2002.

Kaplan, Jane. *Interfaith Families: Personal Stories of Jewish-Christian Intermarriage.* Westport, CT: Praeger Publishers, 2004.

Kaplan, Steven. *The Beta Israel in Ethiopia: From Earliest Times to the Twentieth Century.* New York: New York University Press, 1992.

Katz, Ilan. *The Construction of Racial Identity in Children of Mixed Parentage: Mixed Metaphors.* London: Jessica Kingsley Publishers, 1996.

Katz, Nathan, ed. *Studies of Indian Jewish Identity.* New Delhi: Manohar Publishers and Distributors, 1995.

Katz, Nathan, and Ellen S. Goldberg. *The Last Jews of Cochin: Jewish Identity in Hindu India.* Columbia, SC: University of South Carolina Press, 1993.

Kennedy, Randall. *Interracial Intimacies: Sex, Marriage, Identity, and Adoption.* New York: Pantheon Books, 2003.

Kessel, Barbara. *Suddenly Jewish: Jews Raised as Gentiles Discover Their Jewish Roots.* Hanover, NH: University Press of New England for Brandeis University Press, 2000.

Kessler, David. *The Falashas: The Forgotten Jews of Ethiopia.* New York: Shocken Books, 1985.

Khanga, Yelena with Susan Jacoby. *Soul to Soul: A Black Russian Jewish Woman's Search for Her Roots.* New York: W.W. Norton and Company, 1992.

Kibria, Nazli. *Becoming Asian American: Second-Generation Chinese and Korean American Identities.* Baltimore: Johns Hopkins University Press, 2002.

Kincheloe, Joe L., Shirley R. Steinberg, Nelson M. Rodriguez, and Ronald E. Chennault, eds. *White Reign: Deploying Whiteness in America.* New York: St. Martin's Griffin, 1998.

King, Desmond. *Making Americans: Immigration, Race, and the Origins of the Diverse Democracy.* Cambridge, MA: Harvard University Press, 2000.

Kirk, H. David. *Shared Fate: A Theory and Method of Adoptive Relationships.* Port Angeles, WA: Ben-Simon Publications, 1984.

Klatzkin, Amy. *A Passage to the Heart: Writings from Families with Children from China*. St. Paul, MN: Yeong and Yeong Book Company, 1999.

Klein, Daniel, and Freke Vuijst. *The Half-Jewish Book: A Celebration*. New York: Villard, 2000.

Korgen, Kathleen Odell. *From Black to Biracial: Transforming Racial Identity among Americans*. Westport, CT: Praeger, 1998.

Krementz, Jill. *How It Feels to Be Adopted*. New York: Alfred A. Knopf, 1982.

Landing, James E. *Black Judaism: Story of an American Movement*. Durham, NC: Carolina Academic Press, 2002.

Langman, Peter F. *Jewish Issues in Multiculturalism: A Handbook for Educators and Clinicians*. Northvale, NJ: Jason Aronson, 1999.

Lazarre, Jane. *Beyond the Whiteness of Whiteness: Memoir of a White Mother of Black Sons*. Durham, NC: Duke University Press, 1996.

Lee, Stacey J. *Unraveling the "Model Minority" Stereotype: Listening to Asian American Youth*. New York: Teachers College Press, 1996.

Leslau, Wolf. *Falasha Anthology: Translated from Ethiopic Sources*. Translated by Wolf Leslau. Vol. 6. New Haven, CT: Yale University Press, 1951.

Lester, Julius. *Lovesong: Becoming a Jew*. New York: Arcade Publishing, 1988.

Loury, Glenn C. *The Anatomy of Racial Inequality*. Cambridge, MA: Harvard University Press, 2002.

Lowenstein, Steven M. *The Jewish Cultural Tapestry: International Jewish Folk Traditions*. New York: Oxford University Press, 2000.

Malcioln, Jose V. *The African Origin of Modern Judaism: From Hebrew to Jews*. Trenton, NJ: African World Press, 1996.

McKinley, Catherine E. *The Book of Sarahs: A Memoir of Race and Identity*. Washington, DC: Counterpoint, 2002.

Melamed, Abraham. *The Image of the Black in Jewish Culture: A History of the Other*. Translated by Betty Sigler Rozen. London: Routledge Curzon, 2003.

Melanson, Yvette, and Claire Safran. *Looking for Lost Bird: A Jewish Woman Discovers Her Navajo Roots*. New York: Avon Books, 1999.

Min, Pyong Gap, and Jung Ha Kim. *Religions in Asian America: Building Faith Communities*. Walnut Creek, CA: AltaMira Press, 2002.

Moran, Rachel F. *Interracial Intimacy: The Regulation of Race and Romance*. Chicago: University of Chicago Press, 2003.

Nam, Vickie, ed. *Yell-Oh Girls! Emerging Voices Explore Culture, Identity, and Growing Up Asian American*. New York: Quill, 2001.

Nash, Gary B. *Forbidden Love: The Secret History of Mixed-Race America*. New York: Henry Holt and Company, 1999.

Nieto, Sonia. *Affirming Diversity: The Sociopolitical Context of Multicultural Education*. 3rd ed. New York: Addison Wesley Longman, 2000.

———. *The Light in Their Eyes: Creating Multicultural Learning Communities*. New York: Teachers College Press, 1999.

O'Hearn, Claudine Chiawei, ed. *Half and Half: Writers on Growing up Biracial and Bicultural*. New York: Pantheon Books, 1998.

Omi, Michael, and Howard Winant. *Racial Formation in the United States: From the 1960s to the 1990s*. New York: Routledge, 1994.

Onolemhemhen, Durrenda Nash, and Kebede Gessesse. *The Black Jews of Ethiopia: The Last Exodus*. Lanham, MD: Scarecrow Press, 1998.

Pact, An Adoption Alliance. *Pact's Booksource: A Reference Guide to Books on Adoption and Race for Adults and Children*. San Francisco: Pact, An Adoption Alliance, n.d.

———. *Pact's Multicultural Book Source*. 2nd ed. San Francisco: Pact, An Adoption Alliance, n.d.

Papo, Joseph M. *Sephardim in Twentieth Century America: In Search of Unity*. San Jose and Berkeley, CA: Pelé Yoetz Books/Judah L. Magnes Museum, 1987.

Parfitt, Tudor. *Journey to the Vanished City: The Search for a Lost Tribe of Israel*. New York: St. Martin's Press, 1993.

———. *The Thirteenth Gate: Travels among the Lost Tribes of Israel*. Bethesda, MD: Adler and Adler, 1987.

Perry, Pamela. *Shades of White: White Kids and Racial Identities in High School*. Durham, NC: Duke University Press, 2002.

Pollak, Michael. *Mandarins, Jews, and Missionaries: The Jewish Experience in the Chinese Empire.* Philadelphia: Jewish Publication Society of America, 1980. Reprint, New York: Weatherhill, 1998.

Prager, Emily. *Wuhu Diary: On Taking My Adopted Daughter Back to Her Hometown in China.* New York: Random House, 2001.

Price, Richard. *First-Time: The Historical Vision of an Afro-American People.* Baltimore: The Johns Hopkins University Press, 1983.

Primack, Karen. *Jews in Places You Never Thought Of.* Hoboken, NJ: KTAV Publishing House in association with Kulanu, 1998.

Rapoport, Louis. *The Lost Jews: Last of the Ethiopian Falashas.* New York: Stein and Day Publishers, 1980.

Roden, Claudia. *The Book of Jewish Food: An Odyssey from Samarkand to New York.* New York: Knopf, 1998.

Rodriguez, Richard. *Brown: The Last Discovery of America.* New York: Viking/Penguin, 2002.

Roediger, David R., ed. *Black on White: Black Writers on What It Means to Be White.* New York: Schocken Books, 1998.

Roof, Wade Clark, ed. *Spiritual Marketplace: Baby Boomers and the Remaking of American Religion.* Princeton: Princeton University Press, 1999.

Root, Maria P.P., ed. *The Multiracial Experience: Racial Borders as the New Frontier.* Thousand Oaks, CA: Sage Publications, 1996.

———, ed. *Racially Mixed People in America.* Newbury Park, CA: Sage Publications, 1992.

Rosenberg, Shelley Kapnek. *Adoption and the Jewish Family: Contemporary Perspectives.* Philadelphia: Jewish Publication Society, 1998.

Rosenbloom, J. R. *Conversion to Judaism: From the Biblical Period to the Present.* Cincinnati: Hebrew Union College Press, 1978.

Ross, James R. *Fragile Branches: Travels through the Jewish Diaspora.* New York: Riverhead Books, 2000.

Rubin-Dorsky, Jeffrey, and Shelley Fisher Fishkin, eds. *People of the Book: Thirty Scholars Reflect on Their Jewish Identity.* Madison, WI: The University of Wisconsin Press, 1996.

Schwarcz, Vera. *Bridge across Broken Time: Chinese and Jewish Cultural Memory.* New Haven, CT: Yale University Press, 1998.

Shafran, Avi. *Migrant Soul: The Story of an American Ger*. Southfield, MI: Targum Press, 1992.

Shapiro, Sidney, ed. *Jews in Old China*. New York: Hippocrene Books, 1984.

Shipler, David K. *A Country of Strangers: Blacks and Whites in America*. New York: Vintage Books, 1997.

Simon, Rita J., and Howard Altstein. *Adoption across Borders: Serving the Children in Transracial and Intercountry Adoptions*. Lanham, MD: Rowman and Littlefield Publishers, 2000.

Simon, Rita J., Howard Altstein, and Marygold S. Melli. *The Case for Transracial Adoption*. Washington, DC: The American University Press, 1994.

Simon, Rita J., and Howard Altstein. *Adoption, Race and Identity: From Infancy to Young Adulthood*. 2nd ed. New Brunswick, NJ: Transaction Publishers, 2002.

Smelser, Neil J., William Julius Wilson, and Faith Mitchell, eds. *America Becoming: Racial Trends and Their Consequences*. 2 vols. Washington, DC: National Academy Press, 2001.

Sobol, Richard. *Abayudaya: The Jews of Uganda*. New York: Abbeville Press Publishers, 2002.

Sowell, Thomas. *Barbarians inside the Gates and Other Controversial Essays*. Stanford, CA: Hoover Institution Press, 1999.

Spencer, Jon Michael. *The New Colored People: The Mixed-Race Movement in America*. New York: New York University Press, 1997.

Spencer, Rainier. *Spurious Issues: Race and Multiracial Identity Politics in the United States*. Boulder, CO: Westview Press, 1999.

Spickard, Paul R. *Mixed Blood: Intermarriage and Ethnic Identity in Twentieth-Century America*. Madison, WI: The University of Wisconsin Press, 1989.

Steinberg, Gail, and Beth Hall. *Inside Transracial Adoption*. Indianapolis: Perspectives Press, 2000.

Takaki, Ronald. *Strangers from a Different Shore: A History of Asian Americans*. Revised ed. Boston: Little, Brown and Company, 1998.

Tatum, Beverly Daniel. *Why Are All the Black Kids Sitting Together in the Cafeteria and Other Conversations About Race*. New York: Basic Books, 1997.

Tinberg, Thomas, ed. *Jews in India.* New York: Advent Books, 1986.

Tizard, Barbara, and Ann Phoenix. *Black, White or Mixed Race?: Race and Racism in the Lives of Young People of Mixed Parentage.* London: Routledge, 1993.

Tobias, Sigmund. *Strange Haven: A Jewish Childhood in Wartime Shanghai.* Urbana, IL: University of Illinois Press, 1999.

Tobin, Gary A. *Opening the Gates: How Proactive Conversion Can Revitalize the Jewish Community.* San Francisco: Jossey-Bass, 1999.

Tobin, Gary A., and Katherine G. Simon. *Rabbis Talk About Intermarriage.* San Francisco: Institute for Jewish & Community Research, 1999.

Tweed, Thomas A., and Stephen Prothero, eds. *Asian Religions in America: A Documentary History.* New York: Oxford University Press, 1999.

Walker, Rebecca. *Black, White, and Jewish: Autobiography of a Shifting Self.* New York: Riverhead Books, 2001.

Warner, R. Stephen, and Judith G. Wittner, eds. *Gatherings in Diaspora: Religious Communities and the New Immigration.* Philadelphia: Temple University Press, 1998.

Wertheimer, Jack. *A People Divided: Judaism in Contemporary America.* Hanover, NH: University Press of New England for Brandeis University Press, 1997.

Wilkinson, Sook and Nancy Fox. *After the Morning Calm: Reflections of Korean Adoptees.* Detroit: Sunrise Ventures, 2002.

Williamson, Joel. *New People: Miscegenation and Mulattoes in the United States.* New York: New York University Press, 1984.

Windsor, Rudolph R. *From Babylon to Timbuktu: A History of Ancient Black Races Including the Black Hebrews.* Atlanta: Windsor's Golden Series, 1969.

Wright, Marguerite A. *I'm Chocolate, You're Vanilla: Raising Healthy Black and Biracial Children in a Race-Conscious World.* San Francisco: Jossey-Bass, 1998.

Wu, Frank H. *Yellow: Race in America Beyond Black and White.* New York: Basic Books, 2002.

Wuthnow, Robert. *After Heaven: Spirituality in America since the 1950s.* Berkeley: University of California Press, 1988.

Wynter, Leon E. *American Skin: Pop Culture, Big Business, and the End of White America*. New York: Crown Publishers, 2002.

Xu, Xin, with Beverly Friend. *Legends of the Chinese Jews of Kaifeng*. Hoboken, N.J.: KTAV Publishing House, 1995.

Xun, Zhou. *Chinese Perceptions of the 'Jews' and Judaism: A History of the Youtai*. Richmond, Surrey, UK: Curzon Press, 2001.

Yoo, David K., ed. *New Spiritual Homes: Religion and Asian Americans*. Honolulu: University of Hawaii Press, 1999.

Zack, Naomi, ed. *American Mixed Race: The Culture of Microdiversity*. Lanham, MD: Rowman and Littlefield Publishers, 1995.

———. *Race and Mixed Race*. Philadelphia: Temple University Press, 1993.

———. *Thinking About Race*. Belmont, CA: Wadsworth Publishing Company, 1998.